DEATH FROM THE SKIES

THE ZEPPELIN RAIDS OVER NORFOLK

19 JANUARY 1915

By R.J.Wyatt

1990

GLIDDON BOOKS
Norwich, Norfolk

In Remembrance of

Martha Mary Taylor
Samuel Alfred Smith
Percy Goate
Alice Maud Gazley

Who were killed on the night of 19 January 1915

First published 1990 by Gliddon Books

©Copyright R.J. Wyatt 1990

ISBN 0 947893 17 2

Cover design by Abacus '88

Produced by Abacus '88, Bury St Edmunds, Suffolk.
Printed in Great Britain by Ipswich Book Company Ltd, Ipswich, Suffolk.

Introduction.

Dozens of contemporary newspapers and magazines, and some more recently published books, record the story of the first Zeppelin raid over England, they do so with varying degrees of accuracy, each one using virtually the same basic material but placing emphasis on those aspects with which the authors were most concerned or which were seen to be the most appropriate or sensational at the time.

The recent acquisition of a pamphlet written by Holcombe Ingleby, the Member of Parliament for King's Lynn, one of the Norfolk towns attacked on that night in January 1915, led me to read all of the accounts that I could find in my own library and to check all of the primary sources again. Some of the material had not been used before, some of it had been mis-quoted or misinterpreted, some of it seemed to have gone unnoticed; I decided to collect together most of what seemed important and to offer this research project as a small tribute to those innocent Norfolk souls who were unfortunate enough to have been killed or injured as a result of the first air raid on England.

The research has been aided by many people, and I am particularly grateful to the staff at the Public Record Office in Kew, those in the Photographic Department at the Imperial War Museum, Catherine Clinton at Great Yarmouth Library, Mr Lake at King's Lynn Library, Mrs Edna Madle of Snettisham, Percy Goate's cousin and Brian and Jan Gadd of King's Lynn, who helped me with many of the illustrations from their extensive post card collection.

Crown-copyright material in the Public Record Office is reproduced by permission of the Controller of Her Majesty's Stationery Office.

R.J.Wyatt.
Wokingham.
January, 1990.

Illustrations

Top left:	Mr Ellis in front of St Peter's Villa
Top right:	Damage caused to the house
Bottom:	The restored house today
Top:	Mr Pestell's premises
Bottom:	The restored building today
Top:	The entrance to Drakes Buildings, 20 January 1915
Bottom:	The same house today
Top:	Miss Taylor and Mr Smith – the first casualties
Bottom:	The water tower on Fish Wharf

Top:	The crater near Snettisham church
Middle:	Tennyson Avenue – Lynn's first bomb
Bottom:	The train shed
Top:	Scenes from a postcard
Middle:	Bentinck Street – the fatal bomb
Bottom:	The next morning
Top:	East Street, Albert Street
Bottom:	Young Tom Walden peers into the crater
Top:	Mr Wyatt's allotment in Cresswell Street
Bottom:	Headstones to Mrs Gazley and Percy Goate

Contents.

Chapter 1.

The Threat from the Air.

Great Britain declared war on Germany on 4 August 1914, by the end of that month the battle of Mons had been fought and the British army had retreated to Le Cateau and beyond. Things had not gone at all well. On 25 November Prime Minister Asquith wrote to the King (1) giving his customary report on the proceedings of the Cabinet and mentioned that Mr Churchill, who was the Minister responsible for Naval affairs, had reported that a daring raid by airmen upon Friedrickshafen had resulted in the wrecking of the hydrogen factory and probably in damage to one of the Zeppelin ships. Attack as the best form of defence seemed to have been the Admiralty's policy. A few aeroplane raids on England were made late in 1914, one by a seaplane over Dover in daylight on 21 December in which two bombs were dropped 400 yards out to sea and another on Christmas Eve, again during the day and at Dover, which resulted in the first bomb being dropped on English soil; it left a ten feet wide, four feet deep crater in a garden near the Castle and broke some windows.(2)

On Christmas Day, a third aeroplane got as far as the London docks but caused no casualties or damage. These three attacks showed to the Germans the poor state of England's defences against air attack. Airships might present larger targets, but they could outclimb aeroplanes and there seemed nothing to oppose a successful raid, certainly if the aeroplane's example was anything to go by. At this point, it is worth mentioning that England had been bombarded before, not from the air, but from the sea.(3) On 16 December 1914 five German ships bombarded Hartlepool, Scarborough and Whitby killing 142 and injuring several hundred more. Another reason why, in addition to those referred to later, Lord Fisher, the elderly First Sea Lord, must have felt so helpless, and when he might well have imagined that his Navy was letting the country down. However, it is the first airship raid that concerns us now.

Admiral von Pohl had recommended sending airships to attack parts of London of military importance, and military establishments on the lower reaches of the Thames, in January and February 1915 when the weather conditions were likely to be most favourable. The Kaiser took some convincing and the Imperial decision was that London should not be bombed at present but that attacks should be confined to docks, arsenals, and military establishments, even Aldershot provided that no Germans were known to be there at the time. Churchill said (4) that British Intelligence was so good that reports of von Pohl's proposals reached us before the Emperor saw them. On 1 January 1915 Churchill reported to the War Council on the German intention to attack London with airships "on a great scale at the earliest opportunity." It was reported that there were twenty airships capable of reaching London, each able to carry a ton of high explosive, in fact the figures were an overestimate as there were only eight or nine ships available at the time, and each could carry only around half a ton. There was no known means of preventing the airships coming, "I must make it quite plain that the Air Department of the Admiralty are quite powerless to prevent an attack if it is launched with good fortune and in favourable weather conditions." A paper from the Director of the Air Department was attached (5) showing that London was protected by only eight 3 inch guns, forty Hotchkiss 6 pound guns, twenty 1 pound Pom-Poms left over from the Boer War and fifty-three searchlights. There were forty aeroplanes and sixteen seaplanes at Felixstowe, London and Dover districts. Lord Fisher wrote (6) to his old friend Admiral Jellicoe late in December 1914 confirming his belief that when the hard frosts came the Zeppelins would "come over in the dark hours and massacre London." He knew that there was nothing to prevent them. On 4 January 1915 he wrote to Churchill, his political master, reminding him of the reliable information that the Admiralty had on 26 December that a large scale attack was likely. He was worried that the public had no knowledge of the possibility and Fisher was deeply concerned over the bombing of London, particularly as there was no defence, and as no measures had been taken he asked to be relieved of his post on the grounds that the Admiralty would be held responsible for the massacre due to its unpreparedness.

One of the First Sea Lord's proposals to Churchill, and one can only assume that he meant it to be taken seriously, was that we should - "take a large number of hostages from the German population in our hands and should declare our intention of executing one of them for every civilian killed by bombs from aircraft." Churchill, on the other hand, felt sympathy for German nationals held here, he had been a prisoner of an enemy himself in the Boer war, and "urged publicly a merciful attitude towards them", he was, therefore, "offended to receive from Lord Fisher the official minute", and wrote to him on the same day - 4 January - telling him to mind his own business! As he had no professional experience of aerial defence (and on reflection one wonders now who had) and as killing prisoners in reprisal for an attack was not for him to consider, Churchill would take the letter only as an expression of his feeling of exasperation at Britain's powerlessness to resist. Fisher did not reply, but he says that he withdrew his resignation because he was convinced by "authority", presumably Churchill, that the War Office would be held responsible in the event of a raid on unprepared Britain, and not his beloved Admiralty. Churchill must have had some sympathy with that view as his previous utterances made sure that he too could not be blamed. Neither of them seems to have mentioned the matter again. Fisher's fears can be understood when it is considered that historically the sovereignty of the Navy had not been challenged successfully for some 300 years. Here was a threat albeit from the air, which the Navy could not oppose, they had no effective defences against airships and most of the airships were operated by the German Navy. Why had he done nothing about it, he may well have asked himself, after all it was the Navy's job. In assuring him that it was the Army and not the Navy who would be held in default, even though this may not have been true at the time, Churchill removed Fisher's immediate fears. At a meeting of the War Council on 7 January (see Appendix 1) the statement was made again that the Admiralty had reliable information that an attack would soon be made, first by the German Naval Zeppelins on some east coast town, and subsequently a combined attack by Naval and Military airships on London. The War Council decided that no further action should be taken.

Coast reconnaissances by airships were known to have been carried out before the first raid. (7) As early as 15 December 1914 the SS *Ape* en route from Hull to Yarmouth saw an airship flying low and going towards Mablethorpe at 4.10 pm. It was either L3 or L4. It was raining and the weather was calm and misty and it was more likely that she was lost than attempting a raid. On 10 January some airships were reported to have left Belgium to carry out a reconnaissance of the English coast but, possibly because of a strong wind, they returned to base.

What sort of things were they, these early airships? Count Zeppelin built his first airship in 1900 at a time when only balloons and kites took to the skies, it differed from the former in being of rigid construction consisting of an aluminium alloy framework covered with fabric holding seventeen separate bags filled with hydrogen. If some of the bags were damaged, the remainder would keep the ship buoyant. The first machine was over 400 feet long, 38 feet in diameter and driven by two petrol engines housed in gondolas suspended beneath. It could crawl through the air at 16 mph and it contained 400,000 cubic feet of the highly inflammable gas, hydrogen. It flew three times before it had to be broken up owing to Zeppelin's Company running out of money. It had proved itself, and several others followed - one being ordered by the German Army - LZ4 - but it burst into flames in a storm after flying some 340 miles. By 1914, the airship was a proven practical means of transport, even though so many of them were destroyed by fire, but the Army believed in them only in a scouting and reconnaissance role. The Imperial German Navy, however, saw them as aerial bombing machines; under a brilliant leader, Peter Strasser, who flew on many of the missions with the most junior and inexperienced of his airship commanders and who was killed in August 1918 when the ship L70 was shot down in flames over England, and in spite of setbacks, the Germans persisted with the airship. Their first one, L1, had nearly 800,000 cubic feet of gas inside its 518 feet long by 48 feet diameter frame; with three engines to propel it at 47 mph. It was a huge success doing 900 miles in 30 hours, but it crashed at sea in a storm claiming the first fatalities in an airship.

L2 was ordered in 1913; it had to be large enough to carry bombs to England, that meant nearly a million cubic feet of hydrogen powered by four Maybach engines. That, too, met with disaster on 17 October 1913. Freiherr Treusch von Buttlar Brandenfels was there. We will hear more about him later, but he left us with this record which says everything about the danger of trying to operate with a million cubic feet of a highly inflammable gas. (8)

"The engines began to buzz, their hum grew even shriller and shriller; sharp words of command were drowned in the uproar, and at last came the great moment, when the ship, with a lift of a couple of hundredweights or thereabouts, rose into the air and swiftly climbed to a height of a thousand feet or more. Those of us who had stayed behind stood staring up at her, following her with our eyes as she glided on her way.

We could recognise the men looking out of the cars; the flag flapped sharply at the stern.

She must have been about 1,500 feet up, but with the help of glasses, and even with the naked eye, one could still see quite well what was going on. For instance, we could see one of the crew trying to climb from the catwalk into the forward engine car; we could see him quite plainly. 'The trap-door from the catwalk to the engine car has been opened,' observed one of the onlookers who was standing by me. 'But no one is getting down. That's funny.'

Then we saw a terrible sight; our blood ran cold. As we stood looking up, stiff with horror, we saw a long thin tongue of flame leap from the forward engine car along the catwalk.

If only - if only it does not! - Our breath froze on our lips! Our brains were turned to stone! Our staring eyes were fixed on that form in the heavens as the crawling seconds that seemed an eternity passed by.

Then suddenly there was a terrific explosion, the whole sky seemed to echo and re-echo with it. In the twinkling of an eye the airship, from stem to stern, was a mass of flames. Down, down, she came! Then buckling in the middle, she broke in half and crashed to the ground near Johannisthal.

In a trice we all came to our senses. Officers and men, high and low, hastened helter-skelter to the scene of the disaster. So fast did we run that the air seemed to cut into our lungs. We stumbled and fell, but, scrambling to our feet again we dashed forward. Suddenly we were stopped by a light paling. How could we possibly get over it? Three of the Grenadiers who were standing in front of it were evidently asking themselves the same question. 'Come along, you fellows !' I cried to them. 'Throw me over!'

They understood. I was seized by six mighty fists and swung to and fro. Then over! The seat of my trousers must have missed the top of the paling by a hair's breadth, and, describing a fine parabola, I landed on the other side. In my flight, I caught a glimpse of the burning frame of the airship. I staggered towards her.

There she lay before me, a vast smouldering skeleton of wire and steel, sending thick black clouds of smoke curling up into the blue sky. Men were standing about helplessly, staring at her not daring to approach. 'Come along,' I cried 'There are some of our chums in there!' But still they stood staring helplessly. On I went, almost choked by the fierce breath of the devilish flames blown towards me by the breeze.

I noticed that some of the men had tied their handkerchiefs over their nostrils and were trying to approach the wreck. I followed their example but I could feel the heat singeing my eyelashes and eyebrows as the petrol flared up in a miriad thin tongues of flame, hissing and spluttering at the rescuers who were trying to rob them of their victims.

A Pioneer Company, which happened to be on duty close by, ran to the scene of the disaster, and immediately began to attack the inferno of fire and flame with spades, crowbars and shovels. But in spite of superhuman effort all they were able to extricate from the wreckage was mangled and mutilated bodies. True in one or two of the poor charred frames there was still a faint flicker of life, but even as we laid them on hastily improvised stretchers they breathed their last. One of the men we managed to get out was a Lieutenant in the Grenadiers. Where had I seen him before ? Yes, of course! He was in command of the two companies which had come to the aerodrome to hold the airship. He was Lieutenant von Bluel, who had been allowed to go as a passenger in the airship. He died the same evening in a hospital in Berlin."

Twenty-eight men had perished that day.

What sort of men were these Zeppelin aviators ? An allied view, quite likely to have been biassed, came from Lewis Freeman, (9) an American who was a war correspondent with the Allied Armistice Commission in 1918; according to him the typical German airship flyer was hard, fit and capable-looking, he was "......hard, cold (with) steady eyes, the same aggressive jaw, and the same wide, thin lipped mouth that had predominated right through the officers we had met.....". The steady eye and firm jaw were characteristic of most successful flyers but it was the "hardness, not to say cruelty, of the mouth which differentiates the German from the high-spirited, devil-may-care air-warrior of England and America." The Zeppelin pilots - except for von Buttlar - were "mainly of generous girth, with the typical German bull neck corrugating into rolls of fat about the backs of their collars." ! So much for an Allied view of the men.

What of their organisation? Buttlar tells (10) how the outbreak of war came as a complete surprise to the totally unprepared Airship Detachment of the German Navy; on the announcement they scoured the local shops in Hamburg for tinned food. They lacked an officer of sufficient seniority to command L6 when it arrived; this is why, according to Buttlar, such a junior officer as he was put in command at Nordholtz - "the most God-forsaken - one might say the most man-forsaken - hole on earth", and would explain why Strasser felt he should accompany him on the early raid.

Before they risked crossing the Channel, and before authority was granted to raid England, Antwerp had been attacked from the air on the night of 24/25 August - only a few days after the war had started - and again on 2 September, causing a number of deaths.

At the time of the first raid, the German Naval Airship Division had taken delivery of a further six M-Class Zeppelins: L3, L4, L5, L6, L7 and L8. Their Maybach engines gave them a top speed of around 50 mph, they could climb to 5,000 feet and they could carry between 1,100 and 1,430 pounds of bombs. Kapitan Leutnants Hans Fritz in L3, Count von Platten in L4 and Heinrick Mathy in L5 set off from Fuhlsbuttel to raid England on 13 January but, owing to heavy rain, the flight was abandoned over the sea and they returned to base.

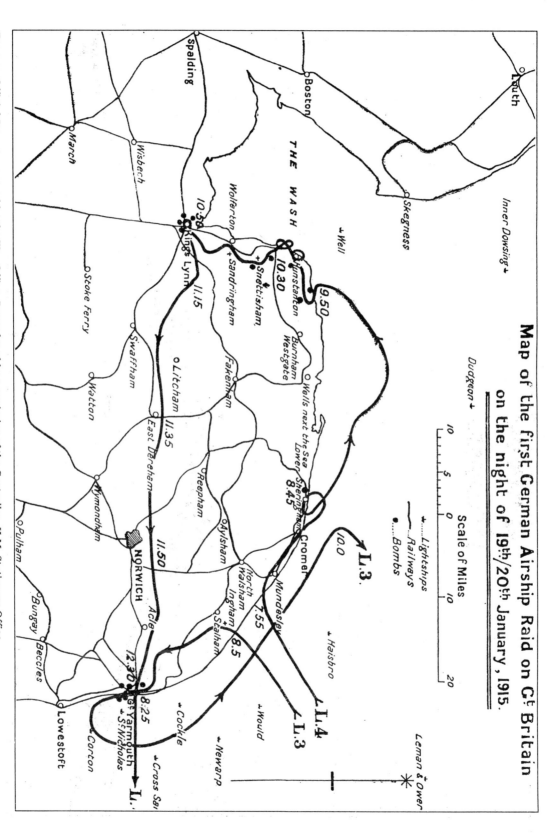

Map of the first German Airship Raid on Gt. Britain
on the night of 19th/20th January, 1915.

Scale of Miles

+....Lightships
—....Railways
•....Bombs

From an Official Report prepared by the War Office. Reproduced by permission of the Controller, H.M. Stationery Office. Map of Airship's routes.

Bomb-run over Great Yarmouth

Chapter 2.

The Raid begins - Great Yarmouth.

Weather conditions were all-important to airships. They had to travel at night to avoid detection, they needed a high cloud base; if there was a wind it needed to be light and in the right direction. A cold, frosty night was quite suitable, but a bright moon had to be avoided. Barometric pressure needed to register about 30 inches. (See Appendix 2).

The earlier flights had been carried out on nights when the barometer was low and the weather was generally unsuitable. Barometric conditions on the night of 19 - 20 January were more favourable. At the outset, pressure was at 30.4 inches, the wind was a moderate South-Westerly, the sky was overcast and it was misty and raining, conditions not considered suitable in later raids because the target was not visible and it was difficult to locate anything. Over the sea, all they had was guesswork aided by a compass that was liable to freeze, and over the land recognition of rivers and other natural features or railway lines and lights from towns at night. Spies guiding the airships to their targets, thought likely at the time, have proved to be without foundation, the amazing stories current in 1915 are dealt with in a later chapter. Accurate forecasting was no better then than it sometimes appears to be today; over East Anglia that night there was a depression - 29.25 inches - the wind was light and from the South-South-West and it was overcast, later becoming fairer and frosty.

On the morning of 19 January, just before 11 am, crewed by 16 men, armed with eight 110 pound explosive bombs and ten or eleven 25 pound crude incendiary bombs and trimmed with ballast to a precise buoyancy, carrying enough fuel to sustain them for thirty hours in the air, L3 and L4 left Fuhlsbuttel on the Elbe just North of Hamburg (now Hamburg Airport) on what Strasser had described as a "distant mission to the West". If we were to believe the author of *Der Kreig Zur See:* (22) "Their objective was the coastal town of Great Yarmouth," which "according to the British Monthly Army List", was a legitimate target because it was part of the "coast defences." A number of "facts" recorded in that book are erroneous; as we will see later, this is pure fiction, if not a deliberate lie.

L6, with von Buttlar in command and Strasser in attendance, left from the "God-forsaken" Nordholtz near Cuxhaven on the coast between the Elbe and the Weser at 9.38 am. This was to be the prestige attack, for L6 led by a junior commander and with Strasser on board, was to attack the Thames estuary but when "half-way over" according to the account in *Der Kreig Zur See,* but in the official German records at 2.45 pm North-East of the Dutch island of Terschelling, just under 100 miles from the English coast, with only two engines left and with freezing rain forming a layer of ice on the airship's covering, Strasser decided "in agreement with the commander of L6, but with a heavy heart, to turn back." London was saved that night.

In spite of what was said in *Der Kreig Zur See,* the two other raiders thought that they were on their way to bomb the North-East coastal towns and to fly up the River Humber. L3 set off from Fuhlsbuttel at 10.45 am (09.45 GMT) and L4 at 10.05 am (09.05 GMT). The Deck Log of L3 records that it was freezing and calm when they took off, the temperature being 28.4 degrees F (about four degrees of frost); with engines at full speed the ship climbed to 1,000 feet where the temperature had dropped to 24.8. She steered a course of 282 degrees and at that height reduced the engines to half speed. By now it was misty and it had started to cloud over; as the clouds developed, Fritz took L3 up to 2,600 feet and at 3.15 pm he changed course slightly to 276 degrees. Keeping in the clouds he passed Terschelling at 4.15 pm. The air temperature was just on freezing point for the rest of the journey. Nearly eleven hours had passed, travelling at between 40 and 50 mph, in the bitter cold in those unheated, freezing gondolas suspended below L3 when, at about 7.40 pm (British time), expecting to be over the North-East coast of England, Fritz spotted land.

Mr J.F.Perfitt was giving military training to the Happisburgh and Brunstead detachment of the Norfolk Volunteers in Mr Ben Slipper's barn at Happisburgh Hall. In 1963 he recalled that after he had dismissed the parade he left the barn and noticed an unusual light in the sky above the tower of Happisburgh church and he could see that it was a Zeppelin by the reflection on the underpart of the airship. It moved off in the direction of Great Yarmouth. A contemporary report in the *Yarmouth Mercury* of 23 January 1915 tells how a resident of Martham "vouchsafed some very curious and interesting information concerning the German air marauder's movements across the Flegg country". He thought that the vessel must have crossed the coast at Horsey (about seven miles South of Happisburgh, which is slightly at variance with the view of Fritz himself and from Mr Perfitt and all other sources which suggest that Happisburgh was the precise point at which L3 crossed the coast), it came across Horsey Mere and Hickling Broad towards Martham, which had a church with a tall spire, with which L3 nearly collided. L3 is said to have hovered around the parish for about half an hour. "Oh if we had only had an aircraft gun we could easily have accounted for it". There was no military authority to inform to give a warning to Yarmouth so the informant watched open-mouthed as something was dropped that burst into a light and burnt steadily in the air. (According to the writer of *Der Kreig Zur See* Fritz recognised Happisburgh lighthouse by the "light bomb which was dropped by his airship" before passing over Winterton.) It lit up the ground all around. Next day, a metal tube, all that was left of the light, was picked up in a lane near Martham Hall: "It was about two feet long and three and a half inches in diameter. At one end, which was solid except for a sort of turn-screw in the centre, were the figures 6, 12, 15, 18, at even distances around the edge, and there were various German words on the tube itself".

Mr Peter B.Cory, the Master of Rollesby Workhouse, a short distance from Martham, said: "I was sitting in my room at about 8.30 and heard a roaring noise - a sound quite out of the ordinary. I rushed upstairs, put my head out of the window, and called out to the Matron, 'Here's a German raider'. I saw a light burning in the sky which cast an illumination on the ground. It seemed to be suspended in the air and was detached from the airship, which by this time was some distance away towards Ormesby, heading for Yarmouth. I judged when it was over the town, as I saw some lights again and two or three flashes. I did not hear the report, but I heard afterwards a bomb was dropped in Mr George Humphrey's meadow, three quarters of a mile away from the Water Works, and next morning a piece of it was picked up". This incendiary was the first bomb to be dropped in the raid. The site was a water-logged paddock near St Michael's church, a lady said that the airship was so close to the ground that she thought it was going to land - she admitted that she made that judgement from the sound of the engines alone, as she could see nothing in the sky ! Mr R.F.E.Perrier, who lived at Ormesby St Michael said that he heard the airship distinctly. A week later the *Yarmouth Mercury* for 30 January reported that there was little doubt that the airship came in from the sea between Horsey and Happisburgh, as it was seen by the cyclist patrols on the sand dunes near Eccles Gap.

For whatever reason, innacurate navigation, faulty compass or change of wind direction, which forced them seventy miles South of their target, the two Zeppelins arrived at the Norfolk coast about the same time. There is no record which suggests that they kept together during the voyage, they certainly would have found it difficult to have kept contact in the dark. It is suggested in Castle's book (11) that L3 knew she was over Norfolk and sent a wireless signal confirming identification but that L4's commander thought the ship was over the original target area in the North-East, and his wireless message to base later reported that he had successfully bombed "fortified places between Tyne and Humber"; as we shall see later, he was at King's Lynn ! This suggests that, other than visual contact, means of communication between L3 and L4 was non-existent.

Fritz claimed that he recognised Happisburgh and the light house at Winterton, whether or not it was at that stage that he signalled his correct position or after he had identified Great Yarmouth is not clear. It is somewhat of an academic point and the truth of the matter is that he was able to identify a particular part of the coastline unknown to him, in the dark by the flashes from a navigation light, all from the light of a parachute flare. A remarkable achievement.

An observer at Ingham, about one and a half miles inland reported that he saw both ships very low out to sea at 7.40 pm and reported upon their lights as being "like two bright stars moving apparently thirty yards apart" (7). One could argue that the two lights were on the same ship, after all, the Intelligence Section report did state mistakenly that von Platen was in command of L3, so it was subject to recording errors, but the report is quite clear and states that the lights separated, one coming inland over Happisburgh -L3- and L4 making Northward along the coast in the direction of Bacton. A German account gives L4's time of passing over the coast, at about the same place, some forty minutes after L3 was seen. Remembering that it was dark and that the population had no experience of air raids, confusing, contradictory reports are hardly surprising. All in all, it does seem that L3 and L4 were unaware of each other's positions after it became dark, that L3 crossed the Norfolk coastline forty minutes earlier than L4 and, miraculously, the commander was able to gauge his exact location. If Fritz was clever rather than simply lucky, then von Platen was inept ! Two ships with the same flight plan, both effected by the same sudden change of wind direction, can safely be assumed to have been likely to have made landfalls at approximately the same place and at about the same time.

The official record reports L3 over Ingham at 8.05 pm Martham ten minutes later, it was reported seen between Acle and Filey at 8.20 and to the South of Caister two minutes after. Within about three miles of Great Yarmouth she headed towards the sea then turned immediately South-West over the town. The first explosive bombs to land on England from a Zeppelin were then thrown out. It was 8.25 pm.

Fritz says that he dropped a second parachute flare when he sighted the town at 8.20 pm, he reported that a battery fired shells at the flare, but that the dazzling illumination hid him from the ground. Reports in the local papers did mention that the sound of rifle shots had been heard and in the *Yarmouth Independent* for 23 January it was said: "in a Northerly direction a brilliant flash from a searchlight appeared in the sky and streamed down upon the town, by this means the raiders perceived they were over a town of some sort and immediately discharged their bombs." The first thing that the residents of Great Yarmouth knew about the raid was at about 8.30 pm when those who lived in the North of the town heard an unusual buzzing sound in the sky, gradually growing more and more distinct. It sounded like a deep, loud aeroplane engine. They had heard them before because there had been an active aircraft station covering nearly five acres on South Denes, near the old racecourse, since it was commissioned on 15 April 1913; it was not particularly active, however, on the night of the first raid on the town. Close to the sea wall one of the original oblong brick buildings still stands, at the edge of the secure lorry park, where it now serves as a Council store house.

People in the streets gathered in groups and looked up in the direction of the sound. A sudden bright flash followed immediately by a dull roar was seen towards the sea front. The machine had skirted along the sea-line and as it approached the recreation ground it turned South-Westerly over the town - ten minutes later it had gone. Contemporary reports are confused about the number of bombs dropped, *Der Kreig Zur See* says six high explosive and seven incendiaries, Cole and Cheeseman agree (2) the official British report (7) gives nine high explosive bombs over the town and no incendiaries, and the deck Log of L3 suggests six 110 lb out of the eight on board and nine 22lb incendiaries out of the ten loaded, Castle (3) agrees with these figures. Morris (12) says they dropped seven of the nine bombs on board. The Ballast Sheet for L3 (cited in 24) proves that there were on board eight 110 lb bombs, ten 22 lb bombs and three 11 lb "light bombs" - the flares. It is possible that some of the 22 lb incendiaries were dropped, failed to explode, buried themselves in the soft ground and were not discovered; there was also some confusion on the ground as to which was an explosive and which was an incendiary. As will be seen from the reconstruction below, which has been distilled largely from contemporary reports and from the evidence of photographs taken at the time, it was not uncommon for these early missiles to fail.

Bomb 1 . There seems no doubt that this was an incendiary bomb and that it fell, "with no great sound", in a water-logged paddock on Mr George Humphrey's Farm at Little Ormesby. A report in the *Yarmouth Mercury* of 30 January states that on the morning after a search the place where it exploded was found; it was well away from the main road and church, and was reached by crossing the farm premises, a sodden wheatfield, through a pit and over a ditch. On the further side there was a hole " a foot and a half across. The broken turf had been thrown up all round, and there were the burnt remains of some chemical like magnesium on the edges. The hole had filled with water, and the missile had penatrated so deeply into the soft marshy ground that a long stick pushed down did not reach anything solid. It was all water and 'slub'. Probably at the bottom there is a portion of the bomb. The upper part was cast by the explosion a short distance from the hole. It is now in the possession of Police Constable Woodman, and is in shape like an iron saucepan with a handle across it as a pail would have. A piece of twisted sheet metal was also found hard by.......... As we left the farm we passed old Mr Humphrey now well over 90. Strange too, that he should have lived all those years to come at the end in peril from a bomb brought many miles through the air over sea and land. His 90 years have seen wonderful things, but this last must be the most wonderful of all.......". After the parachute flare, it is possible that this bomb was released to act as a beacon. There is no doubt that it was a 22 lb incendiary bomb.

Bomb 2. This was the first bomb to fall on the town. It landed on to the lawn of Mr N.R.Suffling's large house, No 6 Albemarle Road overlooking the Wellesley Recreation ground near Beach Railway Station (now the Coach Station). The private green to the rear of the house is known as Norfolk Square and the bomb struck the lawn at the back about three feet from the window at the side of the tradesman's entrance. It buried itself in the ground about a foot deep, leaving a crater two feet in circumference, it split open with a loud report ("a flash and a loud roar" according to another eye-witness). It did no damage apart from splashing mud onto the house. Mr Suffling kept the split case of the bomb as a souvenir. Again, there is no doubt that this was a 22 lb incendiary.

Bomb 3. An explosive bomb which fell onto the concrete pavement at the rear of 78 Crown Road. It did not explode and it weighed 108 lbs, was 23 ins high and 40 ins in circumference when it was dug out next morning by National Reservists and taken to the Drill Hall nearby, to the delight of a large number of visitors who were able to see it on Wednesday 20 January after it was made safe before being taken away by the experts who defused it. It was dirty white in colour and appeared to be made of a metal something like zinc. According to the report in the *Yarmouth Mercury* on 23 January "A weighty object evidently fell near Gordon Terrace [off Crown Road] and exploded, a hole being made in the ground and some metal casing being found. Very little damage was done by it". It struck the gatepost of Mr W.F.Miller's stable yard and "dug a deep hole". The large bomb that was photographed several times being held by Reservists was incomplete, and the assumption was that the damage to Mr Miller's gatepost was caused by the substantial missing portion.

However, it does appear that another part was dug out of the hole in the pavement behind 78 Crown Road later on. Mr and Mrs Osborne, the elderly couple who lived at 78 were "naturally terribly alarmed", "Mrs Osborne was about to go out to do a little shopping, and was just crossing the little back yard to the back door, when the diabolical thing fell with a terrible noise. 'It was like a big gun', she told us, still shaking at the thought. 'It was awful. if I had gone just a step or two further I must have been killed by it'. Mr Osborne said he had been about a good bit, but he never experienced anything like that. He was coming down the hall, when his wife rushed back, and he just caught her in his arms as she fell, fainting. The house was filled with sulphur".

Mr Eley, the landlord of the Crown Hotel, told the reporter from the *Yarmouth Independent* the next day that when the bomb was thrown it appeared, when near the ground, to divide into two parts and emit two brilliant flashes of light. "The damage to the two places mentioned was simultaneous, and he considered that there were either two bombs or that one broke in two parts, and this caused the missile not to explode. As it was the bomb or part of one, buried itself in the road at the entrance to the stables and scorched part of the bottom of the swing doors. There was a large hole left in the ground. Mr W.Miller told our representative that his sister-in-law and her daughter were standing at the door of their residence in close proximity to the place where the bomb dropped, and had a narrow escape. They were very much frightened and immediately and with great thought went indoors instead of rushing into the streets as many did at the first notification of alarm. He added that he was at the Regent Theatre at the time and at once left. He concluded that part of the propeller from one of the bombs had been picked up and also the cap and this probably accounted for the fact that this bomb did not explode. They have been kept as momentoes of the occurrence". A photograph appeared later in 1915 (14) showing a young teenage girl beside a soldier standing in front of a tall gate with some broken stones and what appears to be a shallow hole in the surface of the ground. Displayed before them on a table were three pieces of metal, a cone-shaped piece about four inches across and three inches tall, a tubular canister about eight inches high and five inches in diameter and a small circular plate. The caption stated: "This bomb dropped in the corner (to the left) only two feet from Miss Elsie Miller (who is shown here) and her mother, but it did not explode. It was dug up by this soldier". Mr Eley said that his house was absolutely shaken and it seemed as if the whole place had been struck. Had the shell exploded his house and others must have been wrecked. It is surprising that a hundredweight of metal falling on to a pavement, without exploding, should have shaken Mr Eley's substantial premises. Possibly two bombs fell, an explosive one which failed to detonate and a smaller incendiary; but I favour one bomb which broke in two either on or just before impact.

Bomb 4. This was the bomb which caused the greatest damage in Great Yarmouth that night, and which produced the first two deaths in England by bombs from the air. St Peter's church is a Victorian structure in what was then a relatively poor part of the town, struggling to support its vicar, the Reverend W.McCarthy, its tall tower standing above the surrounding buildings and no doubt acting as a beacon for an attacking airship. It thrives today, not as a Protestant church, but less familiarly for members of the Greek Orthodox faith, to which, no doubt, it owes its survival. Most of the houses around it, in St Peter's Plain, Drake's Passage, Lancaster Road, York Road and St Peter's Road still exist in more or less their original forms, except where the destruction was so bad that they could not be repaired, as was the case with Mr Pestell's premises.

In *The Times* (13) mention is made of the Drill Hall, about fifty yards away from where the bomb fell, as likely to have been a possible target because a Company of the National Reserve was stationed there. It had a glass roof which "although reduced in transparency by a coating of paint, is still far from opaque, and must have afforded a good target for the raiders". Whether those in L3 saw the church or the lights from the Drill Hall is not recorded.

"The scene on St Peter's Plain was one of considerable ruin", said the reporter of the *Yarmouth Mercury* next day. Windows were blown out, tiles were blown down, and walls and woodwork shattered in every direction and the roadway outside St Peter's Villa, Mr Ellis's house where the bomb fell, was covered with debris. (The house was rebuilt and now displays a plaque signifying: "The first house in Great Britain to be damaged by a Zeppelin Air Raid. 19th January, 1915"). Near there, at the entrance of Mr Pestell's office, lay the "shockingly mangled" body of Martha Mary Taylor a seventy-two year old spinster who lived at No 2 with her twin sister Jane Eliza. Her clothes had been torn off and as her face was uninjured it was not apparent that she was dead until she was moved, when it was found that there was a large wound in the lower part of her body. Part of one of her arms was blown clean off and lay in the road near her. National Reservists from the Drill Hall placed her body on a stretcher and took it to the hospital. A Doctor - not Dr Leonard Ley of Alexandra Road who gained notoriety as the first surgeon to operate on an air-raid victim when he removed a bomb splinter from the chest of Pte. Poulter, a Territorial soldier, who was wounded near the lavatory to the East of St Peter's church; he had it mounted as a tie pin - he was examining her when the Reservists reported that the body of a man had been found on the same spot. The hospital ambulance rushed off to recover the other body, that of a fifty-three year old shoemaker - Samuel Alfred Smith - of 44 York Road whose shop was close to where the bomb fell. It appears that he had been standing by his shop's door at the end of a passage having a large double gate one half of which was open, when several bomb fragments struck him. He lay in a pool of blood with part of his head torn away.

Mrs Ellis and the rest of her family were away on holiday in Cornwall. Mr Ellis, a fishworker with Chittleburgh in Northgate Street, was in his back sitting room packing a parcel and two minutes before the explosion he went into the kitchen; had he not done so, it is certain that he would have been killed. The front of the house was blown away and almost everything in it was destroyed, the back outer door was blown off its hinges and fell on top of him, the kitchen window quickly followed. He suffered minor scalp wounds, cuts by glass in the legs, one piece penetrating deeply above the knee.

Mr and Mrs Laws at St Peter's Cottage next door were both out and their windows were all blown in. The windows of Pelhem Cottage - owned by Mr Plowman - next door suffered a similar fate. Both of these buildings were around the corner facing St Peter's church.

On the same side of the road as Drake's Buildings towards the church, was the premises of Mr J.E.Pestell a builder and undertaker, which suffered considerable damage and had to be largely demolished later. Mr Pestell's firm was responsible for erecting the Great War Memorial in St George's Park. He lived on the premises and three of his children aged ten, seven and four were in bed above his office which was on the corner of Drake's Buildings, the roof was blown off above them, but apart from the middle child being covered in rubble, they were not injured. The only casualty was their pet canary who was killed by the concussion.

Windows in the church, at the Parsonage and in York Road, Lancaster Road, Dene Side, King Street and in St Peter's Plain were broken. W.Bacon's blacksmith's forge on the other side of Lancaster Road was bombarded by fragments, all of the window frames were blown out; William Storey at 17 St Peter's Plain was in the back kitchen with his wife, sister, another young woman and his two babies aged two and nine months. They heard the explosion, the house rocked as if it was about to collapse, the gas went out, glass and doors blew in every direction, the women screamed, but when he got the light he found that no one was injured. They were covered in soot and dust. Next door, at No 18, Mrs Scott whose husband had left to join the Army Service Corps at Woolwich on the 18th was alone with her little child of two when she heard the whirr of a propeller, and had she not been dressing her baby she would have gone to the front door. She said: "I think my child saved my life. Then when the gas went out I dropped the babe on the floor in order to get a light again. I had to leave it screaming while I did so". When she lit her candle she saw the destruction - windows, doors, blinds, chairs, pictures, everything was smashed. The baby was not scratched, but Mrs Scott's face was covered in blood from the minor cuts caused by small pieces of flying glass. (The Coroner's report is given in Appendix 3.)

Bomb 5. Not a great deal is recorded about this bomb. It fell a minute or two after the fatal bomb fell into the stables owned by Mr William K.Mays, butcher, at Garden Lane, Friar's Lane near South Quay. The original site has long since been demolished. There was no explosion and the next day the bomb, which was dented where it had apparently glanced into a wall, was found on a truss of hay near a pony in the stable. It was removed to the Drill Hall to join the other unexploded bomb and later taken out to sea, sunk to twelve fathoms and exploded by a time fuse, causing a "great disturbance in the water". It killed a twenty-pound cod which showed its white belly on the surface and was brought home for a meal - the only bomb dropped which served some useful purpose. I assume from the description that it was an explosive rather than an incendiary, particularly in view of the haste to destroy it.

Bomb 6. In Southgate Road, by the Fish Wharf, still stands an empty building which at the time of the raid was *The First and Last Tavern.* A bomb fell outside the building making a "fissure in the roadway" and cracking a granite paving. It was opposite Messrs Woodgate's premises and that of the Yarmouth Steam Tug Company in which "many windows" were reported as having been broken. Two men from the S.S. *Pilot* had a narrow escape and managed to get a child out of danger's way only in the nick of time. Observers claimed that the bomb emitted a "huge, fiery flame" and Mr A.Smith, the landlord of the *First and Last* stated that he had gone to his door on hearing a loud buzzing noise. After an explosion occurred he ran out and picked up some warm pieces of the bomb. It was not possible to "ascertain the character or dimensions of the missile from this fragment".

It was reported in the *Yarmouth Independent* on 23 January that a man staggered into the Corporation School of Science "quivering with excitement and stated that a bomb had fallen a few feet away. He was given restoratives by Mr Crickmer, which revived him, and he was able to go home" (Presumably in a straight line !). There was another report that this bomb scattered a lot of grey substance onto the houses. A week later, two young chaps from the Pilot boat *Patrol*, which was nearly hit in Beeching's Dock (Bomb 7) said that they were on their way to the Hippodrome when they encountered the incendiary explosion on Southgates Road. One had his coat buttons ripped off and the other had a hole cut through his trousers, and the rubber heels of his boots burnt away. It seems certain that this bomb was an incendiary which failed to ignite.

Bomb 7. An incendiary bomb which cut through the dock gates of Beeching's South Dock, and flooded it, seems to have been the next device to have landed. At the time, the drifter *Mishe Nahma* was across the dock entrance and was moored, being repaired after a recent fire on board; the Pilot boat *Patrol* was in the dock. The bomb fell between the two vessels eight feet from the drifter, striking the river side of the gate, which was hollow and fitted into the mouth of the dock. It cut through two planks and sunk in the river. As the tide was high that night, the water poured into the dock. When it was drained a few days later traces were found of a "hard, dark grey chemical, pieces of which burnt like a roman candle, despite its long immersion. Nothing of the metal covering of the bomb was discovered".

Bomb 8. An explosive bomb struck the stone quay of Trinity Wharf a glancing blow. It did not explode and fell into the river. A Private in the National Reserve was on sentry duty at the quay and was nearly hit by it as it just missed the iron crane turntable at the quay. A diver recovered it later. Nothing further is recorded about this bomb.

Bomb 9. This bomb, which fell at the foot of the Port and Haven Commission's salt water tank behind the Fish Wharf, exploded violently and did considerable damage. As it exploded it brought down an electric lamp standard and made a hole in the granite setts about five feet deep and five feet wide and burst the water main. All the windows in surrounding buildings were broken by either the blast or flying bomb fragments; the water tank, on a brick tower was badly damaged. The worst damage was done to the Fish Wharf Restaurant Rooms, the roof was damaged and all the windows with one exception were broken, no doubt more severe damage would have been done had it not been for the protection afforded by the water tower, which was very substantially built and took the main force of the explosion. Mr Joseph Steel, licensee of the Rooms gave what the *Yarmouth Independent* said was "a graphic account" of what happened. One wonders now just how graphic it could have been when Mr Steel opens by saying: "I myself, was not in the house at the time.....but we heard two loud reports in quick succession. One occurred by the Crossley Red Cross Hospital, another one further down by the wharf, and then there was one about twenty yards from my house.....We found shot, pieces of shell, some of the casing of the bomb and also a kind of cap for the top of it..... I am quite sure that the concussion raised the roof of my house bodily and let it down again....An instance of the terrible force of the explosion is easily demonstrated when I tell you that one picture hanging on the wall of my drawing room was turned face to the wall by the shock!"

He then recounted the thrilling story of his daughter's escape from death: "she was seated in a front room of the house, and right in that portion where most of the shock was felt, playing the piano at the time, and the force of the explosion lifted her completely from the piano stool and planted her a distance away against the door of the drawing room. She escaped miraculously without injury. Then my two boys were fortunate in escaping injury. Had they been in bed, as they usually were at that time of night, they would have been sleeping in a room where glass was strewn all over the bed and floor after the explosion. As the bed is near the window they could not have escaped injury. As luck would have it, on this occasion they were rather late, and were playing with a Meccano downstairs instead of being in bed." Mr Steel estimated the damage at about £200.

Other damage at Fish Wharf was confined to glass and roofing. Glass was strewn on the ground by the river and one piece of shell went clean through the wooden wall of the offices of Norford Suffling's, penetrated the iron safe making a hole an inch in diameter and embedded itself in a wall on the other side. The only injury was to Captain Smith, the Fish Wharf Master, whose hand was cut by flying glass.

Bomb 10. Described in one report as the last bomb, this may be so, but as these last three explosive bombs fell within the space of a minute or so, it is difficult to say exactly which was the last. It did considerable damage to the Steam Drifter *Piscatorial* belonging to Mr Harry F. Eastick, who also owned the *Copious* which was lost with nine lives as a result of a German mine shortly after Great Yarmouth was bombarded from the sea on the previous 3 November. She was riddled with holes from stem to stern, a hole was blown in her quarter, timbers were "started", wire rigging was cut like cotton, the windows of the wheel house

Mr Ellis in front of St Peter's Villa

Damage caused to the house

The restored house today

Mr Pestell's premises

The restored building today

The entrance to Drakes Buildings, 20 January 1915

The same house today

Miss Taylor and Mr Smith – the first casualties

The water tower on Fish Wharf

were blown out, steam pipes and ventilators were pierced with innumerable holes and the woodwork was damaged.

A week later, there was discovered in the third floor of a malting on the West side of Malthouse Lane near the Gasworks in Southtown, a piece of jagged steel bomb casing measuring seven and a half by one and a half inches. It seems to have entered through the slate roof and to have come from the bomb which damaged the *Piscatorial* .

Bomb 11. This is generally thought to have been the last bomb to have been "thrown out" of the Zeppelin. It was an explosive bomb and it fell on the macadam road at the back of the racecourse grandstand (the racecourse, then, was on South Dene) near the Red Cross Hospital. It produced what was said to have been the largest crater of the raid and was photographed at the time, it was a couple of feet deep and about six feet in diameter. Some of the paddock wooden fencing was blown down and some fish baskets were destroyed. A portion of the top of the bomb, with its looped carrying handle, was found next morning together with the body of a large black dog.

In those ten minutes on that cold, foggy wet night in Great Yarmouth, during the attack by L3 on what the German's regarded as a legitimate target, in answer to what was said to be fire from anti-aircraft batteries, small but quite damaging bombs were dropped. They were tiny compared with what was to follow later in the war, but they killed two people, wounded a few more and caused damage costing several thousands of pounds. The population of the town does not appear to have been too bothered about it, they seemed to have expressed active curiosity rather than horror or dreaded fear; the only immediate effect seemed to be the creation of even greater hatred for the foe, with an equal degree of contempt. No doubt it helped the recruiting along too. Criticism was levelled at the Council for not having reduced the street lighting before the raider came over the town, why, they asked, could not the "authorities" have been warned by someone from further up the coast? No answer was given, but some tightening up followed; only open boats were allowed to move on Yarmouth Roads between an hour after sunset and half an hour before sunrise, Evensong in the churches was to start between 3.30 and 4 pm, weekly Saturday night markets had to be given up because lights were prohibited, powerful lights on cars were not allowed and street lighting was reduced.

There was not too much emotion in the local press, but the Nationals made up for it. *The War Illustrated* in its issue of 30 January, under a heading of "The coming of the Aerial Baby-Killers", while agreeing that the damage done was no greater than would have been caused by a gas explosion, went on to say: "the loathsome blood-mad fiends who could do this foul work and rejoice stirred every Briton's heart to sterner resolve to crush that degraded nation whose war methods are more savage than those of the lowest races known to anthropology............Demented Germany is gloating over the proof that their Zeppelins can cross the North Sea and kill English children of four years and English women of seventy". Of course, they went on to say, British airmen could never do such a thing.

According to the report of the British Intelligence Section (7) L3 made off in a North Westerly direction, following the coast to Runton where it turned seawards at 10 pm. According to our friend in *Der Kreig Zur See* the airship left the English coast in rain and fog at 21.27 and landed at Fuhlsbuttel 15 minutes after L4 at 10 next morning. The journey home for them was far from pleasant, the freezing rain built up ice on the envelope; just before he sighted the Dutch coast at 12.45 am the port engine stopped for a short time followed by the forward engine when a fuel line broke at 2.45 am. At 4.40 the starboard engine stopped with two cracked cylinders - they must have been greatly relieved to land in the fog at their home base - after 22 hours and 51 minutes in the air ! These are the official times recorded in the log. L4 landed five minutes later.

Whatever else we might think of the raid, of Fritz and of his crew, it is quite remarkable that, expecting the North East coast, they were able to identify their location in the dark and the cold so precisely, with the aid only of two parachute flares and a map.

What of the remains of poor Martha Taylor and Samuel Smith?

At 1 pm on Saturday 23 January Smith's funeral took place quietly and without publicity, which meant that there was no usual crowd of inquisitive spectators. Lunchtime was chosen and hardly anyone except those immediately concerned were present. The coffin was brought from the mortuary and taken in a hearse past Smith's house in York Road where it was joined by the mourners; his brother from Sunderland, his mother and sister, cousin and niece. The procession passed through the streets to the church, no one being aware of whose funeral it was; the service took place and the body was interred in the Old Cemetery. No headstone appears to have been erected. Miss Taylor had been buried, in a similarly unpublicised way the day before, the public not having been made aware of the event. She was buried at Caister, in Plot Number F842 in the Southern Section of the Cemetery, behind the Chapel. A low kerb memorial is inscribed to indicate that she was one of the first two people to be killed in an air-raid.

AIR RAID ON THE EAST COAST OF ENGLAND

THE FLIGHT THAT FAILED.

The Emperor. "WHAT! NO BABES, SIRRAH?"

The Murderer. "ALAS! SIRE, NONE."

The Emperor. "WELL, THEN, NO BABES, NO IRON CROSSES."

[*Exit murderer, discouraged.*]

Punch cartoon, 27 January 1915

Instruction to Great Yarmouth residents

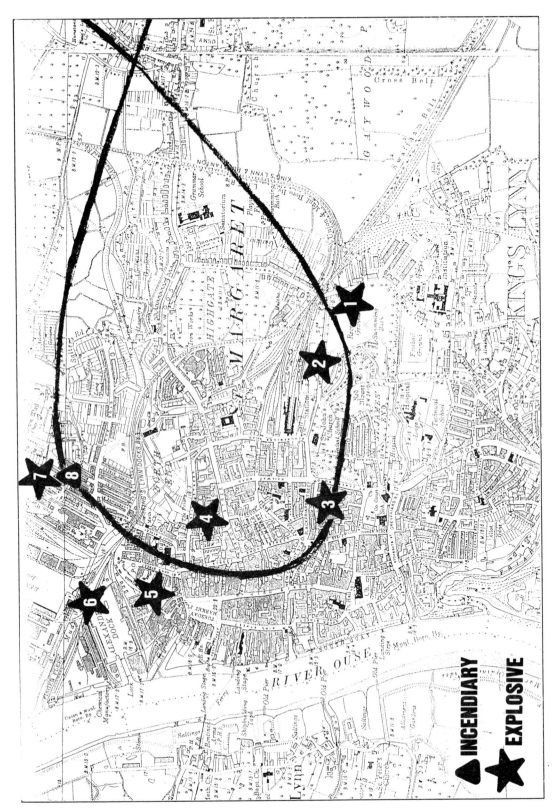

Bomb-run over King's Lynn

Chapter 3.

L4 Attacks King's Lynn - without knowing it !

L4, commanded by von Platen-Hallermund, presents a more accurately documented course, certainly as far as its appearance at King's Lynn is concerned, largely because the report submitted to the Home Office by Charles Hunt, King's Lynn's Chief Constable has been preserved. (15) Assuming that both L3 and L4 approached the Norfolk coast from the North-East together it seems clear that they were not in communication and that they had been out of contact with each other for some time. Whether or not Fritz had made a conscious decision on the way, or only realised that he was over Norfolk after he sighted land, is not clear but the airships both left their base at about the same time - L4 twelve minutes after L3, L4 doing 935 miles in all and L4 1,052, but it seems that they did not cross the coast together, in spite of the one report which states that their lights were seen to diverge as they separated out to sea.

We have seen how clever Fritz had been at locating his position, von Platen seems to have been unlucky or incompetent. L4 headed towards the coast and crossed it at about 7.55pm according to the majority of the reports, in Robinson's *The Zeppelin in Combat* he gives the time from the official German account (corrected to GMT) at 8.30pm. The position seems to have been somewhere close to Bacton. Throughout the whole raid he thought he was South-East of Grimsby; later he claimed that he was fired upon from the ground and that action prompted him to drop his first bombs. Robinson gives this quotation from von Platen himself: " I turned off North, in order to get behind the sea front and to reach and attack the Humber industrial area from the land side. Against expectations, I did not find the North bank of the Humber on a North-Westerly course." One would not expect to on the North Norfolk coast !

L4 followed the coast round to Cromer, over which it passed without realising that town was below, it seems that the place was in darkness. It went out to sea just after it passed the town and circled back inland between Weybourne and Sheringham. It was now 8.35. Within the next ten minutes von Platen brought the Zeppelin down to 800 feet and dropped a flare East of Sheringham and an incendiary bomb into a house in Windham Street which did considerable damage but caused no casualties. Another incendiary was dropped on a building plot 300 yards further on. Close to Beeston Regis, L4 turned North-West out to sea at 8.55 and as far as Sheringham was concerned that was the end of it. After some time over the sea, L4 was not seen overland again until nearly an hour later when it passed Thornham, between Brancaster Staithe and Hunstanton where another incendiary was dropped in a field, (Mr R.Sheldrake of Holme-next-the-Sea wrote to a newspaper many years later and said that it dropped on the Green, known locally as the Eyesore) the airship went out to sea and back over Brancaster to drop another one close to the church. According to the special correspondent of *The Times* (13) (who seems to have been the same writer as the one who reported for *The Lynn Advertiser,Wisbech Constitutional Gazette and North Norfolk and Cambridgeshire Herald* in its issue of 22 January) at 9.50 the airship twice circled round and over the village, turning on a searchlight for a few moments and dropping a "missile containing some inflammable substance" just before it left. It dropped on a road leaving a hole six inches deep about fifty yards from Dormy House and 150 yards from the Red Cross Hospital. That made a total of four incendiaries.

Bomb 5. This is quite an interesting one and was the first explosive bomb dropped by L4. The official report (7) says that it went over: "...Holme-next-the-Sea to Hunstanton, where at 10.15 an HE bomb aimed at the wireless station dropped in a field about 300 yards away. After circling the town, which was in total darkness, it went out to sea twice, but returned each time and then made off along the coast to Heacham....". Contemporary reports from Hunstanton tell us that people there were startled by the unusual sound of an aircraft engine at about 10.30. What the local people imagined was an airship passed over the water tower slowly from the East and followed the shore line to Heacham. No bombs were dropped at Hunstanton and consequently no damage was done, according to reports in the *Lynn Advertiser* on 22 January, which went on to say : "The inhabitants seemed to have taken little more than a mild interest in the passing aircraft, and showed no fear or panic." *The News and County Press* a week later had received a longer report from the representative of the *Lynn News*, he had received estimates from local residents that the airship had been over the town for from fifteen to twenty minutes and goes on to say : "The fact that considerable damage was not done to the town is undoubtedly due to the fact that it was in perfect darkness; not only were public lights out, but the windows of all private residences were darkened." Some weeks before the local Council had decided that all but four street lights should be dispensed with, and on the advice of Superintendent Lewis, the Chief of Police, the leader of the Council ordered that these should also be put out, and residents were advised to darken all windows - it is a pity that the same action was not taken at Lynn, as we shall soon see. L4 flew over the gasworks, the pier and the lighthouse and circled the neighbourhood several times going backward and forward over the sea. Several people saw lights from the machine and some claim that they were quite powerful searchlights, but even so there is no evidence that a bomb was dropped at Hunstanton and although L4 knew it was over the coast-line it seems to have been unaware of having been over a town. In the 1960's there was a report from a Mr Geoffrey Searle that his father found a Zeppelin bomb "where Clarence Road now is".

Apart from in the official report, there is no other mention of a bomb having been dropped at Hunstanton, so it has to be concluded that the fifth bomb was reported in error. Even those questioned for an article in the *Eastern Daily Press* in 1978, one of whom was riding his motor-cycle towards Hunstanton on the night of the raid, could not recall a bomb having been dropped there, although they remembered well the sound of the explosion from the one at Heacham.

Bombs 6 and 7. At around 10.40pm the Zeppelin passed over Heacham. Mr R.Pull of Arcadia went to bed at 10.15 that night, and just afterwards heard what he thought was an aeroplane. He got out of bed and looked out of the window, noticing that the sound was receding. He returned to bed and after a few minutes he heard the noise again and looked out of the window once more expecting to see a British aeroplane. The noise was so unusual, however, that he thought it must be an airship when he saw a flash, followed in two seconds by an explosion and a "tremendous flare of light". When it faded away, in a minute or two, he immediately rushed downstairs ordering the lights to be put out because he thought that the raider was returning. A few minutes later the windows rattled, probably from the effect of the Snettisham bomb.

Two cottages in Lord's Lane, a thickly populated part of Heacham, belonging to Mrs M.Patrick, one of which was empty and the other occupied by her, her daughter and son-in-law Mr T.Allen who both lived with her, had a narrow escape. Mr Allen was, like Mr Pull, looking out of his back bedroom window when the bomb fell; it smashed the adjacent window of the adjoining cottage about six feet away from Mr Allen's window. The bomb just caught the left hand edge of the window sill, broke off the face of some of the bricks in the wall, tore off about a square foot of the tiling and wall of a wash-house adjoining the house and fell into a rain water tub blowing it to pieces. Mr Pull said that the report of the explosion was not the terrific sound that he had anticipated.

On Thursday, two days after the 19th, a lad named Dix was walking across the field owned by Mr Brasnett which was between the council school and the chalk-pit when he found the second bomb, which had failed to explode, embedded in the soil. He reported it and later on two soldiers took it to Homemead where it was placed on the lawn to be guarded and viewed by many people until on Sunday an Officer from Woolwich Arsenal came to take it away. He is reported to have said that it was a very destructive 100 lb bomb which, had it exploded, would have damaged buildings within a 100 yards radius.

Bomb 8.   The next report was from Sedgeford, where people heard the droning of engines from about 9.30 till about 11.00; three explosions were heard there, the last of them at about 10.45 was very loud. At Snettisham the noise of the Zeppelin`s engines was heard towards Heacham and it appears that L4 headed first inland for Sedgeford, but changed course for Snettisham. The Zeppelin was first seen there at about 10.45 near the old Grammar School and appeared to be passing the village on its right, travelling to the left of the church towards Inmere. It hovered over a Mr H.C.Sherringham's premises and headed again for the village which it circled twice before dropping a bomb, the terrific explosion of which shook the whole place. A searchlight was seen shining from L4 as it disappeared towards Lynn. It does appear that the church was a deliberate target, but the bomb missed dropping about four yards from the Sedgeford road in Mr Coleridge's meadows. A contemporary photo shows the type of crater left by one of the smallest explosive bombs. The church was quite badly damaged, nearly all of the South aspect windows were broken, the lower ones and the frames being completely smashed. One window in the vestry was blown in; the organ escaped but tablets and masonry were blown from the walls in the vestry. Some of the windows in Mr Lambert's and in Mr Coleridge's houses, about a hundred yards away from the crater, were broken. On the other side of the church, windows at Sutton Lea, a house 250 yards away, were broken; some outbuildings at Manor Farm and the farmhouse itself had some tiles stripped off.

The only other casualty was an oak tree twenty yards from the hole which lost some branches and had its trunk scarred.

The Reverend I.W.Charlton, the Vicar of Snettisham wrote a report to the *News and County Press* which is quite an interesting social document in itself. It is one of the few not to have been written by a journalist and as it is a statement direct from an eye-witness it is given here in full: "Supposing that the distant noise was the hum of an ordinary aeroplane, and that some lights would be visible, my wife and I and a lady friend were walking about in the garden, trying to penetrate the darkness and discover the aircraft. The drone of the engine was so much louder than usual that we were quite prepared to descry at length, exactly overhead, the outline of a Zeppelin, hovering over the church and Vicarage at a great height, appearing, at the distance, to be only about fifteen or twenty yards long.

No sooner had we identified it as probably a German airship, than suddenly all doubt was dispelled by a long, loud, hissing sound; a confused streak of light; and a tremendous crash. The next moment was made up of apprehension, relief and mutual enquiries, and then all was dark and still, as the sound of the retiring Zeppelin speedily died away.

That there was no loss of life, and that the church (with the exception of 22 windows) escaped damage, we owe, humanly speaking, to the fact that the bomb fell just far enough off all surrounding houses to make the concussion and the splinters almost harmless and also that it fell on a soft rain-soaked meadow, with a hedge and a wall between it and the church."

It appears that the Vicar did not think of extinguishing the lights when his party went outside to "descry the outline" of the raider, for another report says that the windows of the Vicarage were "brightly lighted for the entertainment" !

Dersingham is about two miles South of Snettisham and L4 passed over it before crossing between Wolferton and Sandringham, the Royal Residence (no member of the Royal Family was there that night). A villager there went to bed at 10.40 and almost immediately "through the dead silence, through the open window, came the sound of a purring engine". Quite why he had his window open on a freezing January night we are not told, but this contrast between a sermon-like verbatim report and what the reporter for the *News and County Press* did with the story is worth reading too: " 'Confound it,' I said to myself, 'J....has got stranded in his car and wants to be put up here for the night. That means getting up and finding the matches.' The purring continued for a minute or two and then it got louder. 'A most extraordinary car', I said to myself. Then came a shattering crash at some distance. This was too much. No mishap with the mechanism of a car ever made a noise like that. In a couple of minutes more all doubts had disappeared, for the noise of the oncoming air machine literally filled the parish. One who heard it at dead of night here described it to me as equal to the noise of 200 motor cars, and I am not prepared to say that this was an exaggeration. The airship passed almost directly over my house, and roughly followed the course of the railway line.

I did not see the airship, but a Dersingham friend tells me that he saw it at a height of about 300 feet above his house. It was cigar-shaped and almost as long as Dersingham Station. No lights whatever were showing, and if any orders were being given they were inaudible in the roar of the engines. He estimated that the enemy was travelling at that time at the rate of about 40 mph.

The alarming noise soon caused lights to twinkle at many windows in Dersingham, but volunteers quickly went round the parish warning the people against a possible return of the enemy, and when I traversed the roads at two in the morning only one light could be seen. As indicating the intensity of the darkness one might say that it was difficult to distinguish poplar trees against the sky.

About midnight I met on the roads several groups of people, and I would wish to testify to the remarkable calmness which residents showed in the midst of those most alarming conditions. In the small hours I called at the Police Station, and there found being done everything that could be done, quietly and efficiently by Mr Lewis and his staff. There was, of course, great inconvenience owing to the pressure on the wires.

One reflection passed across my mind. It was this. What would have been the position at Dersingham had bombs been dropped in the parish causing injuries to a number of people? What arrangements has Dersingham made to cope with sudden surgical and nursing necessities?" The answer to the last, of course, was none whatsoever - had a bomb dropped, our reporter would have had something to write about, instead of just filling up his lines !

Before we learn of the detail of what happened at Lynn, one amusing anecdote is worth recording. Sandringham, the Royal Residence certainly was not an intended target, in spite of the fact that the popular press of the day claimed that the entire raid was undertaken with the express purpose of destroying it. One Gracious Lady, however, did not know that von Platen was lost and was most concerned about it all. Queen Alexandra wrote to Lord Fisher from Sandringham on 21 January (16) to say:

"This is too bad, those beasts actually went straight to Sandringham, I suppose in the hopes of exterminating us with their Zeppelin bombs - though, thank God, they failed this time. But they killed and wounded as usual a lot of poor innocent women and children at King's Lynn, I am sorry to say.

Please let me have a lot of rockets with spikes or hooks on to defend the Norfolk coast. I am sure you could invent something of the sort which might bring down a few of the rascals.........Do send me the rockets." I have been unable to locate a copy of the reply.

Von Platen, according to Robinson in his *The Zeppelin in Combat*, saw the lights of King's Lynn "on the dark curve of the Southern horizon"; he was certain now that he was not over the Humber, from the small villages that he passed over he assumed that he was to the North of it. He was heading for the "big city" which he could not identify, but as he had met both "heavy artillery and infantry fire" he decided to attack. Of course, he was not shot at from either the ground or the air. According to our friend in *Der Kreig Zur See* : "By this opening hostility the place in question had itself to thank that the airship defended herself by dropping 7 - 50kg high explosive bombs....". Von Platen needed his excuse, for he was likely to be in big trouble back home for having threatened a Royal Palace !

At 10pm Charles Hunt, the Chief Constable of King's Lynn, heard unofficially that a Zeppelin had been over Yarmouth and Sheringham and had dropped bombs. By then, L4 was over Hunstanton, 16 miles to the North. The street lighting had been reduced by half since the previous October, but Hunt decided to instruct the Electrical Engineer to put out the street lights altogether. Men were put on to it and started switching them out - individually ! - because they were on the same circuits as the houses. L4 was getting closer all the time.

Meantime, Superintendent Hunt contacted the OC of the National Guard, a Major Astley, and the OC of the Worcestershire Yeomanry who were billeted in the town. Nothing more happened until 10.40 when a telephone call came from Hunt's colleague in Swaffham telling him that he had heard of the raid from East Dereham and asking him to spread the news around to the other local forces. He tried unsuccessfully to contact Dersingham, but was able to inform Downham and Wisbech. At about 10.45 the Superintendent at Dersingham got through, and told him that bombs were being dropped there - in the middle of the conversation he heard them himself! This worried him so much that he got the Electrician to throw the master switch and plunge the town in darkness. It was ten minutes to eleven and what followed took - in his own words - "more than five but not ten minutes".

Guided by the lights L4 picked up the railway line when over the Gaywood district. In that area, most of the people were in bed - they quickly got up. The noise increased as the Zeppelin approached. It appeared to travel slowly from the North in a Southerly direction and to go over the Hall on its way to Lynn. Lights were put out and the inhabitants of the Gaywood district watched as the bombs fell. Only a few windows were broken there by the explosions, which were severe enough to shake the houses. After the bombardment, L4 was seen to go Eastward over the parish again.

Bomb 9.(Lynn 1). The first bomb at Lynn fell in a field adjoining the Hunstanton Railway at the rear of Tennyson Avenue where a "capacious hole was excavated", and many windows in the houses in Tennyson Avenue and Park Avenue were broken. At Mr E.Melbourne's house in Park Avenue, one of the ground floor windows was partially dislodged, its lower part being shifted about eight inches, but none of the glass was broken.

Bomb 10.(Lynn 2). The next fell on the allotments which skirted the railway line to the North of the Recreation Ground, here again a hole "large enough to bury a horse" appeared, and some windows were broken. The craters of both of these bombs were photographed at the time.

Bomb 11.(Lynn 3). The site of Bentinck Street where the next, and fatal, bomb fell now houses the car park near the swimming baths between St James' Street and Blackfriars Street. Only the odd Victorian house is left and the original street pattern has gone. In 1915 it was one of the most densely populated parts of King's Lynn, filled with closely packed terraced houses of poor quality. Bentinck Street and Melbourne Street suffered the most and about a hundred houses were destroyed or damaged in the area, with many windows broken in the surrounding streets. It seems that the bomb - and there were reports of two - fell on to numbers 11 and 12 on the West side of the street, the houses, and number 10, were almost entirely destroyed.

Number 12 was occupied by Mr John William Goate, his wife and two children. They were all buried under a heap of masonry and woodwork from which they were freed by a party of soldiers, police and neighbours who rushed to the scene. Goate's four year old daughter Ethel was screaming as they reached her father but he told them to look after his wife and children first. He was pinned under an iron bedstead which had to be cut away in pieces with a hack-saw. Ethel, according to her daughter Mrs Carole Flat, was blown into the fireplace, (as reported in *The Leader* on 5 April 1989) : "she was lucky in that she was not badly injured - she had a scar on her forehead and she must have broken a rib at the time as she had a misplaced rib all her life".

Mr Goate suffered a badly crushed foot, a cut face and numerous bruises and cuts on all parts of his body. He was a fitter's mate at Paul's mill and when questioned the next day he said: "I have three children but one of them was staying with friends. When the affair occurred my wife and I were in bed in one room and the two children - Percy, aged 14, and Ethel, aged 4 in another. My wife called my attention to a buzzing noise and asked me if I thought it was an aeroplane, but I said I thought it was only a motor car. Soon after this we heard the first bomb explode, so I advised my wife to go and put the children's lights out, and she did so. I was standing against the foot of the bed feeling for my trousers when a bomb fell on the house. I gripped the bedstead rail and felt myself slipping through the floor, the bed with me. I was in one room and my wife and children in the other, and we all slipped through into the ground floor and were buried in bricks and mortar and woodwork. I did not lose consciousness at all. I was pinned down with the bedstead across my legs, and I found the more I struggled the further I got down, so I lay still and waited for the people to come and rescue me. Some soldiers came and sawed the timber to get us out, and they had to use a hack-saw to the bedstead before they could release me. They got to me first, but I told them to attend to the wife and children, and as I was pinned down by the bedstead they did so.

I was able all the time to move my head a bit and to raise my hand to my face, and it was fortunate it was so, because I found that as I breathed I was drawing dust and mortar which was filling up my mouth; but I just managed to stop this by drawing my shirt over my mouth. The only thing that really troubled me was that I could hear my wife and baby calling for help and I could do nothing. I can hear nothing about my boy, but I am afraid he is dead, because all the time we were under the ruins I could hear the baby screaming and my wife calling for help, but I heard nothing of the boy, and I think should have done had he been alive".

Mrs Beatty at 2 Bentinck Street was standing against her door and was attracted by the noise. Her husband was out and she was with her daughter and little boy. She claimed to have seen the bomb drop: "I flew in and when I got upstairs the lights were out, and the doors and windows were all blown in. Something came through the wall, we could not get to bed after this. All the house is in a state of confusion. I really believe that two bombs dropped here. The front door was blown clean in and it had to be lifted so that I could get out".

Mrs Wykes, at number 1 - nearly opposite 11 and 12 - said that she was in bed when the first bomb came. Her husband was hurt on the head and had to see a Doctor: "The two holes in the mantelpiece upstairs were made by pieces of iron hitting. There is a hole through the ceiling upstairs and the house is a mass of ruins. When the bomb dropped we all rushed downstairs. The lodger fetched my little boy downstairs. We went to the cellar of a friend of mine across there. Our lodger found a big piece of shell. The pictures were smashed, the furniture scratched, and the ornaments broken...."

At 1a, Mrs F.Peck was in bed when she heard the noise and asked her father what had happened; before he could answer, she was flung across her bedroom, the windows went and there were holes in the bedroom walls. The roof was blown off the stables at the back of the house and one of the stable walls was knocked down.

Mr J.W.Juby lived at number 9 Bentick Street, after hearing a buzzing sound which he thought was a motor cycle he saw a blue light drop down in front of the house and then heard a big crash. "....The two houses next to ours, Mr Fayers' and Mr Goate's, collapsed. Mr Skipper was cut about the face. Our doors flew out and the house is smashed up. It was all done so suddenly. We had just gone to bed. We got the boy and the girl downstairs and we heard the report. There was a terrific sound when the two houses collapsed. They found the boy Goate about midnight, and Mrs Gazley on Wednesday morning. I think she heard the report and ran to the door, and the house collapsed and fell on her. We heard Mr Goate shrieking under the ruins. The boy Goate was more smothered to death than anything else. Two houses are gone and three were wrecked. My house is very unsafe. The curious thing is that we did not get a scratch on ourselves. There is not a whole picture in the house. Our hair was filled with pieces of glass, but we did not get scratched. The most heart rending thing was the people in the street who were shrieking........."

Mrs Guy of 33 Melbourne Street whose house at the back adjoined the backs of the two destroyed houses who was at home with her husband, grown-up son and three children, said: "We were all in bed and we all heard this terrible whizzing row and I said 'What's that ?' I had just said that when I heard a terrific noise. There were two bangs against the front door. The ceilings fell in and the windows went crash. We heard dreadful screams and calls for help at the back. That was all we knew until we could get downstairs. The explosion lifted the bed up. It is a miracle we were not all killed. It sounded as if one bomb exploded at the front of us and one at the back. The doors, which had all been shut, were burst open. The clock was blown on to the floor. The blinds and other things were blown in all directions. Even the children's socks were blown through a window on to a nail".

A number of people mentioned that there were two explosions, and although it seems unlikely, there could have been two in very quick succession.

At the inquest on 21 January, the body of the 14 year old Percy was identified by his uncle Richard Thomas Goate; Mrs Goate's statement was read out to the Jury: "We were all upstairs in bed, me and my husband, and the baby and Percy, when I heard a buzzing noise. My husband put out the lamp and I saw a bomb drop through the skylight and strike the pillow where Percy was lying. I tried to wake him, but he was dead. Then the house fell in. I don't remember any more". When PC John Fisher arrived on the scene that night he found Goate being removed to a house in Clough Lane. Later he arranged for the body to be taken to the mortuary. On examination on Wednesday night, Dr G.R.Chadwick found a lacerated wound one inch long across the front of the nose. There was a bruise on the chest. In his opinion death was caused by shock, the wounds not being sufficient to cause death by themselves. On the death certificates of the two victims the cause of death was given as being "From the effects of the acts of the King's Enemies".

In the house which adjoined Goate's, 11 Bentinck Street, Mr and Mrs Fayers were buried under the debris, from which they were quickly released and rushed to hospital. Mrs Alice Maud Gazley, 26 year old widow of Percy George who had been killed recently in France while serving with the 3rd Rifle Brigade, was sheltering with the Fayers. During the night, Maud's father, Henry William Rowe a dock labourer of 4 Albert Terrace, Gaywood Road found that she was missing and reported it to the Police. At 7.30 the next morning Mr Rowe, and a Policeman named Beaumont set to work to dig amongst the ruins of the Fayers' house and, after half an hour they discovered her body. At the inquest it was identified by her father. He had last seen her alive at Blackfriars Road at 10 o'clock on the night of the raid, he went down Bentinck Street soon after the explosion and went to Rose Cottage, her home in Bentinck Street, in which he noticed that windows were broken. After reporting that she was missing he went to the hospital and at 7 am the next morning learnt from Mrs Fayers, who was still recovering there, that his daughter was in the Fayers' house, which was four or five doors away from Rose Cottage, at the time of the explosion and ran out. Mrs Fayers said that they were having supper together when Mrs Gazley said: "There's a dreadful noise". Shortly after there was a bang and Mrs Gazley rushed out of the house and that was the last she saw of her. Dr Chadwick saw the body on Wednesday. It had bruises to the face and abrasions to the front of the right thigh. She had died from shock.

The other house to be wrecked was occupied by Dan Skipper, his wife and daughter. They were in bed at the time and all escaped with their lives, the two women with only slight injuries; Mr Skipper was more badly hurt and was treated in hospital.

Bomb 12.(Lynn 4). L4 now swung around as it approached the river and turning in a tight circle dropped its next bomb in another area of tightly packed terraced cottages, again mostly demolished now, the area being used as a car park. East Street was on the right hand side of Albert Street as it is entered from Norfolk Street. The houses remaining on the left are similar in style to the better ones that used to stand in this part of the town.

The bomb fell in the yard at the back of the house of the vet and blacksmith Mr T.H.Walden, making a large hole several feet deep and about twenty feet across and leaving his shoeing shop nothing more than a pile of bricks and rubble; it also wrecked the house and his dog kennels. The terrified animals escaped and ran barking around the area. Mr Walden estimated the damage at £450. When the bomb exploded, his son Tom was buried in the bedroom (He was pictured in post cards which were issued within a few days standing proudly on the pile of rubble behind the house), but his father got him out safely. In the next bedroom, his sisters Gladys and May were sleeping, their door was wrenched off, pictures fell from the walls and part of a wall fell down, but the girls were not injured. Mr Walden had been sitting in an armchair by the fire ten minutes before the bomb dropped; later he found that the chair in which he had been sitting had been hurled across the room. He had, however, by then joined his wife in the front bedroom where a chest of drawers was thrown across the bed, the window fell in and they were both lucky not to have been cut by the flying glass.

Next door, at Mrs Thorley's, her daughter, Walden's neice Miss Green and Miss Partlett, a visitor from Hungerford, heard the Zeppelin overhead, they shut the door only to have it blown open again immediately by the blast as the interior of the house was wrecked. Mrs Thorley was bruised and cut about the face, Miss Thorley had two wounds in the right arm and Miss Partlett, the most severely injured, sustained cuts to the forehead and on the back of the head. She was taken to hospital and received stitches.

Roofs and windows were damaged in four cottages owned by Mr Hayes, on the same side of the street, a malthouse beyond them was also damaged as were numbers 23, 24, 25, and 26 in the same terrace. Windows were broken in Albert Street and Albert Avenue and at the Albert Inn. A cast iron mangle wheel was blown through the window of a room next to the office of Mr Hayes (who was a cork-cutter) in Albert Street; in Norfolk Street almost all of the shops lost windows or slates and Mr Misson at 28 said he was in bed when the bomb dropped in Bentinck Street, his shop windows were broken and he turned out his lights at once. He got his family downstairs and they sheltered in the cellar of the Eagle Hotel; he went back to his house to put out a light in the attic when the East Street bomb fell. It shook everything. The fire alarm sounded and he went to the fire and found a piece of iron in his yard that had been blown from Mr Walden's yard by the force of the explosion.

Bomb 13.(Lynn 5). This is the seventh bomb referred to in the Chief Constable's report, it is not mentioned anywhere else. All that is known about it is that it fell "In a garden in the occupation of Mr Kerner Greenwood at the back of his house near the Docks. This was buried in the Garden and no damage done".

Bomb 14.(Lynn 6). The next bomb destroyed the engine house and its two boilers and the hydraulic gear which worked the dock gates at Alexandra Dock.

Bomb 15.(Lynn 7). At the bottom of Cresswell Street (The Chief Constable gave Sir Lewis Street in his report to the Home Office) a bomb fell in the allotment used by Mr Wyatt, it made a large hole (photographed at the time) and blew down some fences and some trees. Windows were broken at numbers 21, 26, 30, 31, 32, 33, 35 to 40, and 45 Cresswell Street. Sir Lewis Street runs parallel to Cresswell Street.

Bomb 16.(Lynn 8). The raider had a parting shot at 63 Cresswell Street, where Mr J.C.Savage's family had a lucky escape; he was sitting reading in the parlour and two of his daughters were in bed when a bomb fell through the roof, into the back bedroom - which was unoccupied - though a tin box and into a basket of linen in the kitchen. It set fire to the bedroom on the way and by the time the fire brigade got there it had been put out by neighbours. It was thought that it did not explode because a part was separated from it as it struck the roof, it was found in the yard of Mrs Creasy's house next door. The conical incendiary bomb about a foot long was found by the police and immersed in a pail of water until it was handed to the Chief Constable, whose photograph holding the object was both sold as a post card and appeared in many of the papers at the time. Ten years ago, Jack Savage, then 94, recalled that he dashed out of his own house in Cresswell Street close by and saw that a bomb had fallen on to his father's roof.

A list was issued of those who were treated in the West Norfolk and Lynn Hospital, with brief descriptions of their injuries. Many more people received minor cuts, but they were treated at home or in some cases in the surgery of their own doctor. Those who went to hospital were:

Mr Goate	Cut face and swollen ankle.
Mrs Goate	Leg damaged.
Ethel Goate	Aged 4, stunned.
Mr Fayers	Cut on head.
Mrs Fayers	Cut on face.
G.Harrison	Back of hand cut by glass.
D.Skipper	Face and head cut.
Mrs Skipper	Injured leg.
G.Partlett	Forehead cut and head wound.
R.Wykes	Cut head.
R.Howard	Face cut in two places.
G.W.Clarke	Cut lip.
W.Anderson	Wrist lacerated.

During the bombing, Chief Constable Hunt could only stand by and wait for calls. He was first called out to Cresswell Street but was not needed there. Next he went over to East Street, but his help was not needed there either. By the time he arrived at Bentinck Street Percy Goate's body had already been removed.

Hunt was not in all that much of a hurry in preparing his report to the Home Office, it was dated the 5th of February, was fairly accurate and contained the results of his investigations into reports of cars signalling to the Zeppelins, that will be dealt with in the next chapter, and may have given rise to the delay in telling the Home Ofice what had happened. They would have known, of course, from the dozens of reports that were circulating. There was none of the secrecy of the 1939-45 raids. The real mystery in the file Air 1 552/907 in the PRO are the telegrams from Lynn, Yarmouth and Norwich notifying the Home Office of the raids - all dated 24 June 1915 ! - over five months later. Perhaps someone was trying to get his files up to date !

On Wednesday, the day after the raid, the Watch Committee of the local Council met and decided that in future the street lamps would all be put out at 8pm, and that an order should be issued to shade effectively the windows of all rooms containing lights. The public was advised that on receiving a warning it was desirable to extinguish all fires - there was no instruction on how best this could be done. At 8pm that night the town was plunged in darkness, and this kept many people indoors.

As was the case in Great Yarmouth, the funeral of the youngest victim was performed without publicity. Percy Goate was buried in Lynn Cemetery on Friday 22 January, accompanied only by the family, the Minister, The Rev E.W.Bremner, a journalist, Police Sgt Beaumont, PC Allcock and a few boys and a girl who were his friends. The coffin left his Great Aunt's house in Sedgeford Street, where it had been taken from the mortuary, at 2pm. His mother and father were still in hospital, aunts, uncles and cousins were there. Percy's remains were laid to rest in the new Cemetery on the right hand side just over a little bridge.

The crater near Snettisham church

Tennyson Avenue – Lynn's first bomb

The train shed

SCENES AT KINGS LYNN AFTER THE AIR RAID. JANUARY 19th. 1915.

Scenes from a postcard

Bentinck Street – the fatal bomb

The next morning

East Street, Albert Street

Young Tom Walden peers into the crater

Mr Wyatt's allotment in Cresswell Street

Headstones to Mrs Gazley and Percy Goate

Mrs Gazley was buried the next day, in a grave next to Percy's, after a service in the London Road Primitive Methodist church; in her case there was a big crowd at the graveside.

On 22 January the Mayor, R.O.Ridley, wrote to the Prime Minister as follows: "In reference to the raid of this town by the enemy's aircraft on Tuesday evening last, the 19th inst., I am directed to inform you that considerable damage was done to property in the town, including property of the very poorest classes. As a result various persons are homeless, and others are suffering greatly in consequence of the loss and damage to their furniture.

I shall be glad of an early intimation that it is the intention of the Government to compensate the people injuriously effected. In the meantime, may I ask that some steps may be taken to relieve cases of immediate necessity ?

I am further to call your attention to the fact that no protection of any kind is afforded to the town against raids of the above description, and I beg to strongly urge that in view of the great probability of further occurrences of a like nature some steps may be devised to deal with them.

I believe that I am fully alive to the difficulties of the situation, and I know that great efforts are being made by His Majesty's Government in connection with the conduct of the war. I do suggest, however, that the matter referred to is of great importance, and calls for some action to be taken".

One Eric Drummond, on behalf of Prime Minister Asquith, did respond quickly in a letter dated 25 January: "I am desired by the Prime Minister to acknowledge the receipt of your letter of January 22nd, and to inform you in reply that it is the intention of the Government to take measures to deal with the damage suffered by reason of the recent air raid on King's Lynn similar to those adopted in the case of the recent bombardment of Hartlepool, Scarborough and other places.

The other matters referred to in your letter are receiving careful consideration".

A German official statement was released on the day after the raid. It was signed by von Behnke, Deputy Chief of the Admiralty Staff: "On the night of the January 19th Naval airships undertook an attack on some fortified places on the English East Coast. The weather was foggy and rainy. Several bombs were successfully dropped. The airships were shot at, but returned unhurt".

After the raid L4 made off Eastwards, passing over Grimston Road Station at 11.15, then turned South East over Gayton and Westacre, East again passing to the North of East Dereham at about 11.35, over Mousehold Heath, to the North East of Norwich at about ten minutes to midnight. Unlike Yarmouth and Lynn, Norwich had taken measures to reduce the lights all over the town (18) and as soon as they heard that a Zeppelin had been seen at

Bacton, they "took precautions". Although L4 had dropped all of its bombs, when it flew to the North of the city the electric lights had been switched off and as much of Norwich was in a valley and protected by the mists of the Wensum and Yare valleys it was invisible. Had Norwich not been so quick to extinguish its lights, maybe L4 would have been guided by them when it crossed the coast at Bacton. If the Electrical Engineer at Lynn had switched his lights off when the first warning was given maybe that town, like Norwich, would have escaped ?

After it passed North of Norwich, L4 was seen at Acle at midnight and out at sea North of Yarmouth before 12.30 am. Next morning three airships were seen off Vlieland, did L6 come out to meet them, I wonder ?. The impression given was that the rendezvous was pre-arranged, presumably so that the trio could make some sort of triumphal entry home, even though one had failed. It is known that the crews of L3 and L4 were specially decorated with Iron Crosses for their exploits, and that subsequently both of the airships were lost in a snowstorm off the Jutland coast on the night of 17 February 1915, after they had set out to look for a British fleet that had been reported off the Norwegian coast. They found the sea deserted and on their way back ran into a gale and were forced down in Denmark. After most of the crews had jumped off the ships soared into the air with the weight reduced, except for four of the crew of L4 who were not quick enough and were never seen again. It is not recorded if they were on the Norfolk raid - if they were it might be looked upon as poetic justice.

L6 caught fire and was destroyed during inflation at Fuhlsbuttel on 19 September 1916.

A few local diarists had recorded the raid. E.R.Cooper of Southwold, quite a way from Yarmouth on the Suffolk coast, wrote of hearing the news of the raid and said that he heard nothing because he was in the house, but a local from South Cove told him later that he was outside and heard quite loud explosions which started all the pheasants crowing in the woods, although it was past 8pm. After this, the drastic lighting regulations came out and orders were issued to Special Constables to make inspections from the church steeple and seek out offenders.

The Vicar of Carlton Colville near Lowestoft, the next town down the coast from Yarmouth, recorded in his diary that the houses in the village were much shaken and on 30 January wrote that the Government had ordered that no lights should be lit in the streets and that those in houses should be so shrouded as to be invisible from outside. There were to be no more evening services as it was thought that the light from a village church might help the navigators in the enemy's airships to identify the place and to act as a guide to a centre of population where they could do damage.

Chapter 4.

The MP's "Spies".

There remain two points to consider, the lack of any defensive measures and the reports of signals from cars made to the airship which attacked King's Lynn.

According to the Intelligence Section report, no anti-aircraft action was taken either by guns or 'planes. As we have seen there was an air station at Great Yarmouth (19) at the time and although three machines were ready they did not attack either airship because they had been "lost from view". Had they been visible it is unlikely that the aircraft could have done much damage to the Zeppelins as their only armament was a rifle fired by the pilot, also they were not capable of reaching the Zeppelin's height. Not a single round was fired during the raid. Some aeroplanes did take off around London because someone thought that the raiders were heading there, full details are given by Cole and Cheesman (2).

Valuable lessons were learnt for the future, East Anglia's defences were strengthened considerably and motorised machine guns and car-mounted searchlights were based at Newmarket. Later a German commander maintained that this isolated raid was both premature and a foolish mistake, serving no reasonable purpose, betraying their hand three months before they were ready. By then we had prepared our defences which made subsequent attacks more difficult for them. They gained little and did nothing to depress the morale of the population, although some of the later raids were much more frightening and effective. Interestingly, Great Yarmouth suffered the first and the last Zeppelin raid. Strasser set off on the first, but did not arrive over England and on the last - on 5-6 August 1918 - he was killed by pilots from the Great Yarmouth Air Station.

There were dozens of spy stories around in late 1914, only one or two seem to have had any substance. Mostly, they were the result of unfounded suspicions directed at German people who had been settled here for a long time, or simply against those who were unfortunate enough to possess German-sounding names. One story recorded by the Essex Territorials (20) concerned strange flashing lights on the skyline. People in Norfolk would have been used to seeing the Northern Lights so one can only assume that the fear of possible invasion, night raids or bombardment from the sea frightened some folk sufficiently for them to report almost any bright lights. They were all investigated and proved to be no more than car headlights appearing on a road which passed over a hill seen for a second or two when going over a crest. 161 Brigade was training in East Anglia at the time of the invasion scare and they were involved in coastal defence work. Armed parties took up positions at dusk on main roads to detect anyone suspected of spying or signalling to enemy aircraft. The road blocks they set up were merely scaffold poles on trestles, but the men had instructions to stop all cars and to record their registration numbers. Nothing seems to have been reported by them.

With hindsight it is apparent that German spies in Norfolk, assuming that they existed, could not have been warned by their masters in advance to enable them to signal directions to airships. That would have assumed a predetermined intention to attack Norfolk but, as we have seen, everything was directed towards the North-East and the arrival over Norfolk was unplanned - in one case the commander was totally unaware of having been there. To many people at the time the question was - how could raiders know precisely where they were on a dark night without help from the ground ? Under the circumstances the fact that there was a spy scare is not surprising. In fact, the episode proved that night bombing by Zeppelins was by its very nature indiscriminate.

As early as 22 January the *Lynn Advertiser* was recording the observations of a Mr. C.M. Winlove Smith of St. Ronan's, Wooton Road which put him, according to the Press, in: "a favourable position for observing what occurred during the raid", his observations: "showed pretty conclusively that a motor car was acting in conjunction with the airship". Mr Smith took an interest, we are told, in airships, aeroplanes and the mechanism of aerial bombs and said to the reporter from the *Advertiser*: "I had been home twenty minutes on Tuesday night when my wife and myself both noticed the window being violently shaken as though by a violent puff of wind. My wife remarked that there must be another gale springing up, but I said that when I came in there was no wind at all, and I could not understand it. Almost immediately after came another gust, so I jumped up from my chair and went outside to see what was happening. There seemed to be nothing doing, but as I turned to go into the house I heard a sound I knew well to be that of an aerial engine. I immediately took precautions to put my wife and family into as safe a place as possible and went out again into the garden, having extinguished all lights".

As the sound grew louder he deduced that it was coming from an airship engine, then he saw the outline of the airship and saw three flashes which: "indicated that three time fuses had been lighted....just before the airship reached me a dark-coloured covered-in car passed along the road from the same direction. It had two enormous headlights, but no side or rear lights. It travelled very swiftly and silently into Gaywood, went a little way up the Gayton Road and then stopped. The airship came on shortly after passing my house its engine was stopped, giving one the impression that the pilot had lost his bearings. Directly after that the motor car came rushing from the Gayton Road and went swiftly towards Lynn. Instantly the engine of the airship was started again and I could see the machine making a circling movement. When it got over what I took to be the Chase the engine stopped again and the airship appeared to circle back past my house and then go on again more in the direction of the town.

Almost immediately after the first stoppage it commenced to drop bombs.....I saw nine flashes....but I cannot say all of them exploded. Over by the Docks the airship appeared to wait again for guidance, for it hovered there quite five minutes, and then it crossed over our house again and sailed off in the direction of Grimston. As the airship came our way the motor car returned, still travelling at a tremendous pace and went in the direction of Knight's Hill. A friend of mine saw what was evidently the same car standing in High Street whilst bombs were actually being dropped in the town. When the airship passed over Gaywood the first time I estimate she was 800 feet up, but on her return she was much lower - not more than 400 feet".

Mr Smith's friend said that he had indeed seen a car with two bright headlights, but no side or rear lights. It came down Norfolk Street outside Tenowath Bros' shop facing South. The lights were so bright that someone shouted for them to be put out. Mr Smith was also of the opinion that if only the Gaywood Crossing had been guarded as it was during the first few weeks of the war things might have been different. He pointed out that this was the only road by which Lynn could be approached from the coast and there was practically no supervision of people using it.

In London Road, Mr W.F.Attwood said that he saw more than one car assisting the raiders. He heard a noise like a traction engine, went outside, looked up and saw: "a small greenish-blue light going towards the South Gates. It was evidently attached to the Zeppelin, but I only saw the airship itself as something resembling a big black cloud; I could not distinguish its outline. The noise and the light travelled Southward, and I lost sight of the light for a time. Suddenly a motor car with four dazzling lights on the front of it came through the Gates, and within a minute the Zeppelin came back. As the car passed the All Saints' Church Room some soldiers came out and shouted 'Put your light out'. The car ran rapidly along London Road and the Zeppelin followed. Then I saw a bomb dropped, apparently the one that fell in Bentinck Street, followed by another close by it. The car kept on its way and I did not see it again. When the Zeppelin returned it was much lower than when I first saw it. I have spoken with a lady, who states that she saw a light such as I have described over South Lynn Station".

The reporter himself, when standing in Whitefriars Road after the airship had gone at about 11.20 saw: "powerful rays cast upward" by what appeared to be a searchlight or very powerful motor car lamps in the direction of Hardwick Road. By 30 January, the *News and County Press* was reporting that the guidance theory was discredited. The Police: "acting under prompt instructions from the Home Office" carried out an exhaustive enquiry into the movements of cars in West Norfolk that night. The Intelligence Section report (7) contained the following statement: "There were a good many reports of signalling to the enemy from motor cars, etc, during the raid and during other raids during 1915. They do not, however, seem to have been substantiated". In his report to the Home Office on 5 February (15) Chief Inspector Hunt, the Chief Constable of Lynn, said that no mention was made by any person at the time concerning assistance given to the raiders by motor cars. None of his Officers received reports of any car or person acting suspiciously. He claimed that it was only after seeing reports in the Press that people began to say what they had seen, enquiries were made and nothing suspicious was found. On the night of the raid a Constable was stationed on Hardwick Bridge on the Downham to Swaffham Road from 10pm to 6am the following morning - poor soul - only two cars passed into Lynn at the time of the raid. One of them, brilliantly lit, carried Officers of the Worcestershire Yeomanry who were returning from dinner at Middleton Hall, some three miles away. There were no restrictions on the intensity of car headlights so nothing was done to reduce the beams from this, or a number of other cars seen in Norfolk that night. He said: "Unfortunately the people who talk of seeing these cars took no steps at the time either to take their numbers or to assist in any way regarding the identification of the cars. In fact no reports were received until the letters appeared in the Press". He, and the adjoining Police forces, were satisfied that nothing of a suspicious nature occurred that night.

Holcombe Ingleby, the MP for King's Lynn was unconvinced. He was sure that there was a conspiracy of silence. It was his firm belief that spies had been responsible for guiding the Zeppelins to likely targets, yet the Home Secretary had assured him in the House of Commons that fears of German spies flashing guiding lights were unfounded. He was still far from convinced, it was his town that had been raided and he was sure that spies were responsible. He challenged the Home Secretary and began to collect "evidence" that cars had been flashing lights and driving recklessly all around Norfolk that night - the local Police, he claimed, had been told not to answer his questions.

He would not let the matter drop and even went to the trouble of publishing a pamphlet which he sold for three pence (21). On Tuesday, a week after the raid, he wrote a letter to *The Times:*

"Having read in an evening paper that the story of motor cars accompanying the Zeppelin during its visits to these parts seems to be discredited officially, I thought it well to pay a second visit to Snettisham and take a more careful note of the evidence. The result is an entire and complete confirmation of the facts stated in my previous letter. Indeed, the evidence is not only overwhelming, but of so far-reaching a character as to appear almost incredible.

I called first on a family living in a cottage on the slope above Snettisham church, and a little more than a quarter of a mile from it. The father had previously told me his story, and now I heard it afresh from the daughter, a very straightforward, intelligent witness, in the presence of her mother and brother. The whole family, including a daughter, who was then absent, witnessed what I am about to relate. To make it clear I ought to state that some 300 or 400 yards above the church to the East is a spot where four cross roads only do not meet because of an awkward kink that prevents their meeting. This is known in the district as 'Sixpenny Hole'. This piece of road lies exactly between the cottage and the church, though nearer the former than the latter. On the night in question the daughter had opened the door to watch for her brother's return, and while waiting she saw a powerful light in 'Sixpenny Hole', which was presently extinguished. Just as her brother came up, they heard the hum of what proved to be the Zeppelin. The daughter suggested that it might come from the motor that had stopped at the place indicated, and which appeared to have broken down. The motor itself was not visible on account of a small copse intervening, and in any case it would have been hidden by the bank overhanging the road.

The whole family now came out of the house, and they saw a number of flashes coming from 'Sixpenny Hole'. The Zeppelin then flashed, apparently in answer, and as it came up the motor flashed once more and disappeared down a lane to the South, which for some way is on a bee-line with Sandringham. I ought to say that up to this point the family had only guessed that the light came from a motor. The grating of the gears as it restarted made their supposition certain. Next door to this cottage lives Sir Edward Green's keeper, a man of considerable education and thoroughly reliable. He entirely confirms the essential part of this story. He took the village constable to look at the tracks of the motor car that had disappeared down the lane".

Ingleby wrote a further letter to the papers asking for information from residents regarding the movement of cars in West Norfolk on the night of the raid..."I know already about the movements of the Rector of Sandringham's car, Dr Roddis' car, and the military car that went for a joy-ride as far as Snettisham station". People were all too ready to respond - as ready as they would have been in the 1960's to confirm reports of visits by flying saucers.

Holcombe Ingleby's "evidence" in the form of letters from anyone who would write to him, begins with a far-fetched report of two men, who because they later shared a double-bed in a hotel room and were rather slow to answer the bedroom door in the morning, he later assumed to be a man, and a woman in disguise! They were dressed in military uniform and were suspect because they: "....attracted attention in the dining room that night by their unmannerly behaviour. They came in late and stood for a long time with their caps on". Despite the suspicion the pair aroused someone agreed to lend them a car and chauffeur in place of the "ramshackle thing" they were driving. Off they went from Hunstanton towards Brancaster where, at Old Hunstanton, they passed a young constable on point duty who they "commandeered"! They were driven to the village of Titchwell where there they had an altercation with the vicar, whose daughter had seen what she thought were suspicious characters in the garden. After a "flood of Billingsgate" language (not from the vicar) the two men became threatening, and accused the vicar of being a spy who they thought should be thrashed. The bluff seems to have worked, quite why the constable allowed himself to be a party to it all is not recorded; perhaps he preferred being driven around in a car than being on point duty. A police inspector interviewed the two men back at their hotel and as no action was taken he must have been satisfied with their identity documents. Holcombe Ingleby tells us that the inspector would have arrested them had they remained "but for instructions from Headquarters".

A lad of 16 told the investigating MP that he saw a bright light flashing upwards from a car a week before the raid, this and similar reports were the basis for the thesis that the Zeppelins were directed by spy-cars on the night of 19 January.

There is a great deal more humour in Ingleby's *The Zeppelin Raid in West Norfolk*; there is no doubt that he was a politician, every denial and every piece of contradictory evidence was used to prove or disprove a point. When the Home Secretary told him that the Zeppelin's visit was believed to be in the nature of an accident or an afterthought, he jumped to the conclusion that this accounted "for the vagaries of some of the motor cars, which were previously inexplicable". Using the reports of flashing lights that coincided with positions at which the airship was sighted, his friend H.C.Sheringham worked out a most unconvincing map of the Zeppelin's course from the East of Hunstanton to Lynn. The pamphlet finishes amidst reports such as the one of the man in the back of a car with a muffler around his head, who had a "fair moustache and looked like a German", and lights flashed from houses and the morse signals which lit up the North Norfolk sky. If they were all done for the benefit of L3 and L4 they failed dismally.

In *The German Air Force in the Great War* by Neumann (23) it was claimed that the raid caused dismay and terror throughout the whole of England and rejoicing in Germany. We have seen that this was an exaggeration as far as Norfolk was concerned. In reality, the Germans never considered that the Zeppelin would have a major effect on the outcome of the War, although they did tend to over-estimate its role in reducing morale. There is no doubt that the raids caused considerable resources to be diverted from the Western Front, in aeroplanes, manpower, guns and ammunition. From the German viewpoint the defences that we had to prepare "almost defied description" - they certainly were a factor.

Only a few people are alive now who can relive that first air raid and they were all very young at the time, I have attempted to gather together all the facts about the event and hope that this will help us to remember the four innocents who died. Rest in Peace.

References.

(1)   PRO CAB 41/35/61

(2)   *The Air Defence of Great Britain 1914-1918*. C.Cole and E.F. Cheesman. 1984. PRO AIR 1 554/16/15/45 lists the raids which took place between 24 Dec 1914 and 1 Mar 1916.

(3)   *Fire Over England*. H.G.Castle. 1982. p36.

(4)   *The World Crisis*. W.S.Churchill. Vol 2 1923.

(5)   PRO CAB 37/123-1

(6)   *Fear God and Dread Nought*. A.J.Marder. Vol 3 1959.

(7)   PRO AIR 1 2123/207/73/2 *The report of the Intelligence Section GHQ GB on Airship Raids from Jan-Jun 1915*. Written in 1916, revised in 1917.

(8)   *Zeppelins Over England*. Treusch von Buttlar Brandenfels. Translated and published in England in 1931. p19.

(9)   *To Kiel in the "Hercules"*. Lewis R.Freeman. 1919.

(10) *Fire Over England*. p10.

(11) *Fire Over England*. p46.

(12) *The German Air Raids on Great Britain,1914-1918*. Capt J. Morris.[1925].

(13) *The Times*. 21 Jan 1915.

(14) *Memorial of the German East Coast Raids and Bombardment by Sea and Air*. A booklet of photographs published in 1915 in Middlesborough, which shows Miss Miller standing beside a soldier with a very small bomb on a table.

(15)   AIR1 552/16/15/38 contains the report to the Home Office written on 5 Feb 1915, and the original telegrams.

(16)   *Fear God and Dread Nought.* Letter 112.

(17)   *The Times History and Encyclopaedia of the War.* Part 79, 22 Feb 1916.

(18)   *Peace Souvenir. Norwich War Record.* [1919]. p40.

(19)   *The Story of a North Sea Air Station.* C.F. Snowden Gamble. 1928. p22.

(20)   *Essex Units in the War, 1914-1919. Vol 5 Essex Territorial Infantry Brigade.* By J.W.Burrows. [1932]. p36.

(21)   *The Zeppelin Raid in West Norfolk.* Holcombe Ingleby. London, 1915.

(22)   *Der Kreig Zur See, 1914-1918.* German Marine Archive, Vol 3. Chapter 5.

(23)   *Die Deutschen Luftstreitkrafte in Weltkeige.* By Neumann, translated as *The German Air Force in the Great War,* by J.E.Gurdon in 1920. p122.

(24)   *The Zeppelin in Combat.* By D.Robinson. Revised Edn 1966.

Appendix 1.

Views of the War Council, 7 January 1915.

Meeting of War Council 7 Jan 1915. The PM drew the attention to the First Lord of the Admiralty's note on the defence of London against airships. Kitchener agreed with the content, Fisher said there was "reliable information that an attack would be made, first by the Naval Zeppelins on some East coast town, and subsequently a combined attack by naval and military airships on London. He thought they would probably wait for still, frosty weather and come at night".

Churchill explained the arrangements for the defence of London. The conclusion of the meeting was that NO FURTHER ACTION CAN BE TAKEN AT PRESENT.

Churchill, in reponse to a question from Lord Crewe asking if the arrangements had been made for warning the civil population of an impending attack so that they might take cover said that "the expediency of this was not certain" but that "the question was being examined"; Which after Fisher's quite firm and positive warning about a likely raid shows that even if he did take the threat seriously he was complacent about what effective additional defence measures could be taken on the ground.

Cited in *Winston S.Churchill,* by Martin Gilbert. Heinemann. 1972 Vol 3 Companion Part 1 p384.

Appendix 2.

Great Eastern Railway Records.

Very early on, precautions were taken by the Great Eastern Railway against air raids because they rightly assumed that London would be the prime target, and that the enemy would get there by flying over the Eastern counties and that railway lines would assist their navigation.

One of the defensive measures they took was to set up a network to report the movement of airships and aeroplanes. These were all marked up with coloured pins on railway route maps in an operations room at Liverpool Street Station. Later on, a series of barometric readings were taken for each day, with the raids plotted on them. These provided conclusive evidence that attacks took place (by Zeppelins in the dark) on a rising barometer with pressure at about 30 ins when the forecast suggested that there would be a "slightly retrograde barometrical reading" on the return journey across the North Sea which would discourage organised pursuit.

A good description of the work of the Great Eastern Railway is given in Volume 1 of E.A.Pratt's *British Railways and the Great War,* 1921 pp 421-434. An article, "Air Raids and the Weather" appeared in *The Times* on 27 Sep 1920.

At the PRO at Kew, PRO RAIL 227/502 contains the book of pasted-in barometric pressure charts referred to, covering the period from 4 Feb 1916 to 30 Jun 1918, with a continuation to 1919. At the appropriate points, at day or night with times during which raiders were over Britain, the sheets are marked to distinguish between aeroplane and Zeppelin. There are no records for 1915.

PRO RAIL 227/503 has 35 plans, marked with routes and times when raiders were seen, bombs dropped and machines destroyed. The maps cross-refer to the barometric pressure charts in 227/502. They start with the raid on 13 Oct 1915 and finish on 5/6 Aug 1918.

Appendix 3.

Coroner's Inquest.
Held at the Town Hall, Great Yarmouth, 21 January 1915.
Borough Coroner: J.Tolver Waters.
In attendance: Fleet-Surgeon Miller RN, Chief Constable Parker.

The Coroner reviewed the facts on the surroundings and concluded that if there had been two missiles the two victims met their ends at practically the same time. They were both loyal subjects of the King and Country and there was no doubt that each death was caused from what was patent to all, the dropping of bombs from an airship that raided the town. Several bombs were exploded in different parts of the town - one on the Fish Wharf, another near St Peter's Church, one fell near the Drill Hall and another in Norfolk Square. One fell close to a pony, marvellously and miraculously in a stable on some straw but did not explode and it had been preserved intact and was in the custody of the military authorities. There was absolutely no doubt that the bombs were thrown from a hostile airship belonging to the enemy of this country - Germany - and that it came here with the purpose of committing wanton destruction and the taking of life, which, according to my mind and that of every reasonable thinking man in this country, was nothing short of murder, plain and simple - (hear,hear). There could be no military object in the visit for no military advantage could be gained.

It had no military significance, and to my mind would not hasten victory for them or defeat for us. First we had the raid by German ships on Yarmouth, and also at Hartlepool, Scarborough and Whitby, where hundreds of lives were sacrificed for no earthly purpose, and one could only feel the wickedness of the whole thing and that it must be simply the last act of despair. As the Germans could not gain their ends on the other side they were endeavouring to bring evil and destruction here if they possibly could. Of course under ordinary circumstances if anything occurred to cause loss of life by anyone's hands that person would rightly hang, but I am afraid in this case we cannot get the right person. The person in question was carrying out the orders of the authority under the Kaiser, there could be no doubt, but at the same time it was none the less murder. It is not right that unprotected and unfortified places like Yarmouth should be open to wicked attacks from the enemy. I have fully thought out the verdict and shall be prepared, after you have heard the evidence to advise you as to the verdict. I am afraid that it will not be possible - as it would be your wish, I am sure - to return one of "Murder". That is out of the question. There is only one verdict we can return under the circumstances. I should like to finish my observations by expressing my sympathy with every inhabitant of the Borough, and also with the relatives of the two victims who have suffered such a grievous loss by the untimely end of these two people.

The first witness to be examined was William Edward Smith, labourer, of 11, Aylesbury Street, Sunderland, who identified the body of his brother Samuel Alfred Smith, a shoemaker of 44, York Road.

Henry John Cox, a Sergeant in the National Reserve, said that his quarters were at the Drill Hall - "On Tuesday night, approximately 8.30, I returned to the Hall after the explosion and took some of my men onto St Peter's Plain in order to keep people back. A civilian came to me and asked if I was in charge of the party and I replied Yes. He said 'There's a man lying dead'. I went to what I call Gouge's Yard and found a dead man there. He was lying with his feet a few inches from the door-way of his premises leading to the road and his head lying well towards his own shop door, which is in the yard. In my own mind I was quite satisfied he was dead. There was a pool of blood against the head and another against the body. I immediately set off for the hospital to fetch a stretcher and I saw Dr Potts, to whom I reported what I had discovered, he coming back to the body before it was moved. By his directions it was taken to the mortuary".

Coroner:	"Where were you when the bomb burst ?"
Mr Cox::	"In the market place".
Coroner:	"Hearing the report you returned to Head-Quarters?"
Mr Cox:	"Yes, the same as all soldiers did".
Coroner:	"Did you think it was a bomb?"
Mr Cox:	"I had no doubt".
Coroner:	"Did you have a look about afterwards?"
Mr Cox:	"Yes, I found a hole 3 feet to 3 feet 6 inches deep and from 25 to 30 paces from where I found the man. This was undoubtedly caused by the bomb. There was a great deal of damage done all round".

Police Constable Charles Brown said: "About 8.30 I was on duty at the top of Regent Street at the King Street end and I was informed that a man was injured on St Peter's Plain. I proceeded there and saw a crowd of people outside No 16a, which is the number of his shop. I enquired if anyone had heard a man being injured, and a man replied, 'Yes, I believe there is a man lying in the passage dead'. It was very dark about there and I borrowed a candle and found Smith lying on his left side. I could see he was badly knocked about and was dead. At that moment the National Reserve ambulance arrived and he was taken to the mortuary. He was lying in a pool of blood when I found him".

Coroner:	"Did you see an airship?"
Brown:	"An aeroplane. I was watching it come over the town. It .came up from the North-East. It was going to the South'ard.It appeared to come over Boots' Cash Chemists and pick up the lights of King Street and then sail right the way over the top of the street".
Coroner:	"Did it look like a Zeppelin?"
Brown:	"No".

Coroner:	"What did it look like?"
Brown:	"More like our own machines".
Coroner:	"Was it very high up?"
Brown:	"Not more than 150 feet".
Coroner:	"Were there any lights shown from it?"
Brown:	"Not until it fired off. I saw lights after the first report. I thought until that it was one of our machines".
Coroner:	"Did you see it sufficiently to say whether it was a Zeppelin or an aeroplane ?"
Brown:	"It was an aeroplane. I could see by the lights of King Street. What made me think he took King Street as his mark was because he altered his course. He appeared to be going straight down the street".
Mr Blyth:	"I suppose we have no evidence from the Air Station as to the lights which can be seen from the town?"
To the Constable:	"In your opinion had there been no lights he would not have seen where he was going?"
Brown:	"I would not say that. If he had not altered his course he would have gone right over to the South-West from the direction in which he was first going".

Sergeant John William Farrant of the National Reserve said: "I heard the explosion and Sergeant Cox came to me and asked me to telephone for the Police ambulance. I was in E Company Orderly room at Vauxhall Station, when I first heard of the aircraft, the sentry rushing in and telling us about 8.15. He said 'An airship is coming over'. I immediately rushed out, got on a car and reached the Drill Hall".

Coroner:	"Did you see the airship at all?"
Farrant:	"No,it was too dark,but I heard the buzzing".
Coroner:	"Can you give any evidence of the description of the bomb?"
Farrant:	"We have no description of the one on St Peter's plain but experts say it was of the same kind as we have- a conical shaped one. The experts say that from the damage done it must have been a conically shaped bomb. During the voyage of the airship over the town, nine or ten bombs were dropped, two or three different classes of projectiles were thrown. The airship came from a Northerly direction and the first bomb was dropped at Ormesby.
Coroner:	"What is the weight of a bomb?"

Farrant:	"An intact one was found in a stable at the back of Friars' Lane. It measured 27 inches from top to base, and width across was 12 inches. The circumference at the base was 40 inches. The weight is 108 lbs, that is with the fuse, cap and propeller".
Coroner:	"Do you know the amount of charge they carry in them?"
Farrant:	"No. I have some stuff which is inside one of the bombs inside the casing was a hard material of darkish colour like a piece of rock, and there was a centre core of a very light substance".
A Juror:	"Could we work it out and see whether one aeroplanecould carry the weight?"
Coroner:	"Is it possible for an aeroplane to carry that weight?"
Farrant:	"Almost impossible for an aeroplane or Taube".
Coroner:	"There must have been several then?"
Farrant:	"Not over this town".
Dr Horace Potts:	"I made a Post-Mortem examination. I found that the top of the man's skull had been nearly blown away, and the brain was stripped from the base on the skull. The left thigh was very extensively lacerated, and almost divided from the body. Death must have been instantaneous".

In the next case, the first witness called was the sister of Martha Mary Taylor: "My sister went out just before 8 o'clock to go to a grocer's in Victoria Road. That was the last I saw of her alive".

Private Alexander Brown, National Reserve: "I stumbled over a lot of refuse in St Peter's Plain, and saw what I thought was a bundle. On closer examination I found that it was the body of a woman. Corporal Hickling, National Reserve, and I removed the body. I was in the Hippodrome when I heard a report which shook the building. We thought it was the Lifeboat gun".

Corporal Hickling:	"I heard the aircraft when I was in my garden in Adam and Eve's Garden. There was a momentary flash like a searchlight and a streak of fire. I saw something like a flash of lightning. It was towards St Peter's church, I put on my tunic and went at once to the Drill Hall. I noticed a great deal of damage had been done on St Peter's Plain".
A Juror:	"Was it near enough for you to hit it with a rifle?"
Hickling:	"I don't know. I did not see it because it was too dark".

HC 157836

CERTIFIED COPY of an **ENTRY OF DEATH**
Pursuant to the Births and **Deaths Registration Act 1953**

Registration District KING'S LYNN

1915. Death in the Sub-district of KING'S LYNN in the COUNTY OF NORFOLK

No.	When and where died	Name and surname	Sex	Age	Occupation	Cause of death	Signature, description, and residence of informant	When registered	Signature of registrar
388	19th January 1915. Bertinck St. U.D.	Percy GOATE.	Male	14 years	Son of John William GOATE of Bertinck Street, King's Lynn Labourer.	From the effects of the acts of the King's Enemies.	Certificate received from H.C. Allinson Deputy Coroner for Borough of King's Lynn. Inquest held 21st January 1915.	Twenty third January 1915	F.A. Bush Deputy Registrar. Registrar.

Registration District KING'S LYNN

1915. Death in the Sub-district of KING'S LYNN in the COUNTY OF NORFOLK

No.	When and where died	Name and surname	Sex	Age	Occupation	Cause of death	Signature, description, and residence of informant	When registered	Signature of registrar
387	19th January 1915. Bertinck St. U.D.	Alice Maud GAZLEY.	Female	26 years	Widow of Percy George GAZLEY. late of Bertinck St. King's Lynn 3rd Rifle Brigade. Killed in France.	From the effects of the acts of the King's Enemies	Certificate received from H.C. Allinson Deputy Coroner for Borough of King's Lynn. Inquest held 21st January 1915.	Twenty third January 1915.	F.A. Bush Deputy Registrar Registrar.

Registration District Yarmouth

1915. Death in the Sub-district of Yarmouth Southern in the County of Great Yarmouth

No.	When and where died	Name and surname	Sex	Age	Occupation	Cause of death	Signature, description, and residence of informant	When registered	Signature of registrar
401	Nineteenth January 1915 St. Peter's Plain U.D.	Martha Mary Taylor	Female	72 years	a Spinster of 2 Drake's Buildings St. Peters Plain U.D.	Injuries to left side, right shoulder, left arm and other injuries caused by explosion of bomb dropped by hostile aircraft	Certificate received from J. Tolver Waters Coroner for Great Yarmouth Inquest held twenty first January 1915	Twenty first January 1915	Lucy M. Peaton Registrar.

Registration District Yarmouth

1915. Death in the Sub-district of Yarmouth Southern in the County of Great Yarmouth

No.	When and where died	Name and surname	Sex	Age	Occupation	Cause of death	Signature, description, and residence of informant	When registered	Signature of registrar
402	Nineteenth January 1915 St. Peter's Plain U.D.	Samuel Alfred Smith	Male	53 years	A shoemaker of 44 York Road, Yarmouth U.D.	Injuries to head and left thigh caused by explosion of bomb dropped by hostile aircraft	Certificate received from J. Tolver Waters Coroner for Great Yarmouth Inquest held Twenty first January 1915	Twenty first January 1915	Lucy M. Peaton Registrar.

Certified to be a true copy of an entry in a register in my custody.

Brenda Burridge   Deputy Superintendent Registrar.
26th April 1989 Date.

47

Constable John
Pumphrey: "On Wednesday morning at 9am I found near the spot where the
                      bomb had exploded on St Peter's Plain the left forearm of a woman. It
                      was lying on some clothing. I took it to the hospital, and was informed
                      that the body of Martha Taylor was minus the left forearm".

Dr Raymond Shaw: "I examined the body on Tuesday night and Wednesday morning. The
                      left side, from shoulder to hip, was opened and the organs practically
                      destroyed. The right shoulder joint and the right knee-joint bone were
                      broken, the region of the right ankle was injured and the greater
                      portion of the right arm was missing. In making the complete Post-
                      Mortem I found no bullets in the body. Death must have been
                      instantaneous".

The Coroner addressed the Jury: "The unfortunate man and woman were victims of so-called
warfare - but I do not call it so. It is the offspring of German culture. It is contrary to
International Law to attack any unfortified place, such as Yarmouth is. But the Germans are
past masters of regarding anything in the form of writing as a mere 'scrap of paper'. They
are not a party to the Hague Convention, but they appear to regard that, too, as only a piece
of paper which could be torn up. It seems now that whether a place is fortified or unfortified
it is now subject to German attack. In the first raid Yarmouth suffered no loss, and in the
second the actual loss, so distressing as it was does not compare with that of Scarborough
and Hartlepool. Still it is none the less sad. I cannot advise you to return a verdict of Wilful
Murder, but following what the Coroners at Hartlepool and Scarborough have done, I advise
that the verdict should be that Samuel Alfred Smith and Martha Mary Taylor received
certain grievous wounds and injuries through a bomb dropped from a hostile aircraft".

The Jury immediately returned a verdict in accordance with the Coroner's advice and
sympathy was expressed to the bereaved relatives.

Both deaths were registered on 21 January and the causes on the Certificates were given as:
Samuel Alfred Smith - Injuries to head and left thigh caused by explosion of bomb dropped
by hostile aircraft. Martha Mary Taylor - Injuries to left side, right shoulder, left arm and
other injuries caused...as above.

Appendix 4.

Lighting Regulations.

Under Clause 3 of the Defence of the Realm Act, by an Order in Council made on 12 August 1914, the power to control lights was given to competent Naval or Military authorities "at any defended harbour to order the extinction, in specified forms, of all visible lights". Five days later, the Home Secretary was given powers to order the extinction or dimming of lights in specified areas. Putting out the lights in London could effect business and restrict traffic movement, so it was decided to reduce the lighting so that it would be more difficult for the enemy to identify his position, rather than to extinguish all lights. In parks it was even necessary to increase the lighting so that the large unlit areas could not be identified, and thereby act as markers.

Requests from the Police to cut out lighting of advertisements, and for shop lights to be reduced went largely unheaded; so on 1 October an Order required all powerful outside lights to be extinguished from dusk to dawn. Street lamps had to be shaded and all other lighting reduced. This applied only to London.

It was not until the end of the year that the restrictions were applied to coastal towns on the East and South Coasts.

Appendix 5.

Letter from Charles Hunt, Chief Constable of King's Lynn, to L.Dunning Esq., HM Inspector of Constabulary, Home Office, dated 5 February 1915. (PRO AIR 1 552/907).

Sir,

I have the honour to report for your information that at 10pm on the 19th January last it was unofficially reported to me that a Zeppelin had been over Yarmouth and Sheringham at 8.30 that Evening and dropped Bombs at those 2 places.

I immediately communicated with the Electrical Engineer of this Borough and asked him to put the street lights out as soon as possible. He stated that his men had started putting them out and he would put further men on and get them out as soon as he could. I may say that the lighting of the streets in this Borough has been reduced by one half since Monday the 19th of October 1914, but it takes some considerable time to put the lights out as the Authorities are unable to turn the Town lights out without extinguishing the lights in private residences, therefore it necessitates men going round and putting each street lamp out.
I at once communicated with Major Astley who is in charge of the National Guard in this Town, also the Officer Commanding the Wocestershire (sic) Yeomanry who are billeted here.

No other information was received by me until about 10.40pm that night when I received a telephone message from the Superintendent of Police at Swaffham telling me of the Air Raid at Yarmouth and Sheringham stating that he had received this information from East Dereham, and asking me to forward it to the Police in the adjoining Divisions. I immediately endeavoured to telephone Dersingham, but being unable to get through to them, I rang up and informed Downham and Wisbech.

About 10.45pm when I was trying to get through to Dersingham the Superintendent there rang me up and stated that a Zeppelin had passed over Dersingham and had dropped Bombs in that neighbourhood. Before a message was complete I heard bombs being dropped close to this Borough. Immediately upon hearing these explosions the Electrical Engineer put out all the lights by switching off at the main, not only putting out lights in the streets but in private residences as well. The Aircraft was soon over our Building and several Bomb explosions were heared (sic) almost immediately.

In my opinion the Raiders were over this Town for more than five but not ten minutes; during that time 8 bombs were dropped and considerable damage to property and persons was done.

Bombs were dropped in the following places viz:-

(1)   In a Field adjoining Railway at junction of Hunstanton and the Norwich line.

(2)   In Allotments adjoining Railway Station within a few yards of where the Royal Coaches are kept.
No particular damage was done by either of these two bombs.

(3)   In Bentinck Street, a thickly populated area, where 2 houses were demolished and a considerable number damaged. One young Man was killed in one house, and in the adjoining house a Woman was killed by the falling of another house. Very few persons were injured in this District many having miraculous escapes.

(4)   In East Street, Albert Street. It fell on a building adjoining a house and did considerable damage to this thickly populated District. No persons were seriously injured.

(5)   This bomb was dropped on a Dwellinghouse in Creswell Street, apparently an incendiary Bomb which did but little damage, no persons being injured although 3 persons were in the House where it actually fell at the time.

(6)   In an Allotment at the bottom of Sir Lewis Street, very little damage being done.

(7)   In a Garden in the occupation of Mr Kerner Greenwood at the back of House near the Docks. This was buried in the Garden and no damage done.

(8)   This Bomb fell on the Power Station of the King's Lynn Docks and Railway Co. doing considerable damage to the Engine room and the surrounding buildings.

During the time the Raid was on the only thing we could do was to stand by and wait for calls. The first call we got was to a fire in Creswell Street, but on arriving there we found that the neighbours had put the fire out, and although the Brigade turned out their services were not required. I next went to East Street, Albert Street where considerable damage was done to property, but found that no persons were injured or required any immediate help. I next went to Bentinck Street where a young man had been killed; his body had been removed before I got to the spot. His Mother had also received slight injuries; his father was buried up to his waist in the debris. With assistance after some hours he was liberated and removed to the Hospital, where he is still detained. His injuries were not of a serious nature, in fact no bones were broken.

Early the next morning a woman was reported missing who was in the adjoining house where the young man was killed. The Police and other people at once set to work in search for her and found her buried the house having collapsed on her, otherwise she was in no way injured.

At the time of the Raid no mention was made by any person respecting any assistance that might have been given to the Raiders by Motor Cars etc. No reports were received from my Officers that any Car or any person in any Car was behaving or doing anything of a suspicious character. After certain reports had appeared in the Press people then began to say what they had seen, but enquiries have been made and in no instance has anything of a suspicious nature been found out. One of my Constables was stationed on the Hardwick Bridge situate on the Downham and Swaffham Road from 10pm till 6am the following day. The only Cars that passed into Lynn about the time of the raid were two. One was conveying Officers of the Wocestershire (sic) Yeomanry who had been dining at Middleton Hall some 3 miles away and were returning home. This Car had very brilliant lights and being a very dark night they showed up very brightly. There was no Order in force at that time to prevent anyone carrying these lights, and as these Officers knew nothing of the raid they naturally took no precautions.

In many other instances reports were made of Cars carrying bright head lights. The occupants not not (sic) knowing that anything was on kept these lights on till they were told to put them out, and many of them drove away without lights.

The National Guard were guarding the Bridges over the Ouse at Lynn and they state that nothing of a suspicious nature passed over the Bridges.

Unfortunately the people who talk of seeing these Cars took no steps at the time either to take their numbers or to assist in any way regarding the identification of the Car. In fact no reports were received until the letters appeared in the Press.

I may say that the County Police adjoining this Borough took steps to trace the ownership of Cars that were seen in their District that night, and they were satisfied that nothing of a suspicious nature occurred in their District.

Some fragments of the Bombs were found after the Raid, and continue to be found. One was handed over to the Naval Authorities, the other pieces which I have now in my possession will be despatched to the same Authorities to-morrow.